There's a **Bobcat** in My Backyard!

There's a Bobcat

The University of Arizona Press

and

The Arizona-Sonora Desert Museum

Tucson

in My Backyard!

Living with and Enjoying Urban Wildlife

Jonathan Hanson

with photographs and drawings by the author

The University of Arizona Press
© 2004 Jonathan Hanson
First Printing
All rights reserved

09 08 07 06 05 04   6 5 4 3 2 1

Library of Congress Cataloging-in-Publication Data
Hanson, Jonathan.
There's a bobcat in my backyard! : living with and enjoying urban
wildlife / Jonathan Hanson.
p. cm.
ISBN 0-8165-2186-7 (paper : alk. paper)
1. Urban animals—Arizona. 2. Wildlife attracting—Arizona.
3. Wildlife pests—Arizona. I. Title.
QL162.H25 2004
639.9'09173'2—dc22
2003020504

British Library Cataloguing-in-Publication Data
A catalogue record for this book is available from the British Library.

This book is dedicated to all those who fight

to preserve open space for wildlife and people

in southern Arizona, whether through research,

contributions, lobbying, direct stewardship,

or—perhaps most potent of all—letters and votes.

Contents

Illustrations

Acknowledgments

I'd like to thank the curators and other members of the staff at the Arizona-Sonora Desert Museum, whose expert knowledge made this book possible. They include but are in no way limited to: George Montgomery, Craig Ivanyi, Mark Dimmitt, Shawnee Riplog-Peterson, Karen Krebbs, Tom Van Devender, Steve Phillips, and Kim Duffek. Among others who shared their knowledge are Ronnie Sidner, David Hardy, and Janice Bowers. I'm also grateful to the superb naturalists and biologists who taught and inspired me through the years: Steve Russell, Charles Lowe, E. Lendell Cockrum, Yar Petryszyn, Chuck Hanson, Bill Calder, and, before any of them, Hal Gras. Everyone at the University of Arizona Press worked hard to make sure this book was a good one. And for her awesome natural history expertise, as well as innumerable other reasons, I'm forever indebted to my wife, Roseann. Finally, thanks to the dozens of people who, when they heard I was writing this book, said "Oh! You *have* to hear about the pack rat/rattlesnake/woodpecker that got into my wife's/brother's/mother's bathroom/attic/air cleaner, and . . . !"

Introduction
Southern Arizona's Urban Habitats

From five thousand feet above ground level, the line where urban Tucson ends and the surrounding desert begins is impossible to pinpoint. Nowhere is there a border with nothing but intact desert habitat on one side and nothing but pavement-skirted brick buildings on the other, a distinct demarcation between concrete and cactus.

Instead, looking out the window of the Piper Comanche, I see a gradual intergrade, from the undisturbed, tawny, pointillist scrub of palo verde, mesquite, saguaro, and creosote, to a scattered house and corral, to one-house-per-five, then one-per-three, then one-per-one-acre lots. Here and there a tract subdivision presents a densely packed block of monochrome, cement-tiled roofs. Then the ordered grid of city streets begins to stamp more of a waffle pattern out of the mix, and soon the central part of town, with its row houses, strip malls, and chain stores, has taken over.

But not completely. As the Piper descends, I can easily follow the courses of the Tanque Verde and Pantano Washes to where they join to form the Rillito River, winding its way through the developed part of town. Along the banks are brilliant emerald blobs of cottonwood trees, but also strips of desert scrub, varying in width from a few feet to a quarter mile or more. Lesser washes pop out of the background, too, both because of their dense vegetation and the disarray into which they force the courses of nearby streets: Alamo Wash, Arroyo Chico, High School Wash, and others, each a ragged braid of mesquite, palo verde, and acacia. I can also see squares and strips and trapezoids of desert that have somehow escaped or been deliberately spared development: the outskirts of Davis-Monthan Air Force Base, some along the Aviation bike path and the Southern Pacific railroad tracks.

Finally, from a few hundred feet up as we turn in to land at Tucson International Airport, I can make out individual yards, in hundreds of which are native trees and shrubs, the tiniest islands of natural habitat within the urban center. My last, most detailed vignette before the aircraft lands is a small flock of mourning doves angling across a vacant lot overrun with desert broom and cholla cactus, while higher up a pair of ravens cruises north, looking for trouble, as ravens always seem to be doing.

The chief purpose of this morning's flight was a photography assignment over a strip of land known to local environmentalists as the Missing Link. It's an area just south of the Rincon Mountains and north of Interstate 10, a mixture of state and private lands thought to be an important corridor for large mammals moving between the Rincons and the Whetstone Mountains to the south of the freeway. The Missing Link is so-called because, in the struggle to preserve the last of Arizona's best wildlife habitat, this relatively small strip is the only gap in an otherwise unbroken mosaic of protected land that reaches from the Mexico border, north through the Rincon and Santa Catalina Mountains, east to the Galiuro Mountains, up through the Gila National Forest, and all the way up to the Mogollon Rim.

Only in the past few decades have biologists and game managers begun to realize that the traditional strategy for maintaining healthy populations of wildlife—setting aside chunks of undeveloped land—addresses but part of the issue. The seed of the inspiration and revelation behind the new strategy came from a seemingly unconnected source: a 1967 book titled *The Theory of Island Biogeography,* by Robert MacArthur and Edward O. Wilson, which dealt with animal populations on oceanic islands.

MacArthur and Wilson studied islands of different sizes and differing distances from the nearest continent, the rate at which those islands were colonized by new species (birds flying there, mammals and reptiles floating over on logs, seeds blowing or carried by animals, etc.), and the number of species, or diversity, each seemed to be able to sustain. What they found, to criminally simplify their work, was that large islands nearest continents had the most colonists, and were able to sustain the largest number of species, while the smallest islands farthest away from continents received the fewest new species and sustained the smallest diversity. They noticed many other characteristics, too, such as that large islands were more likely to support large animals in addition to small ones, while smaller islands had only small species. Also, the more isolated islands were mainly colonized by highly mobile species: birds, of course; plants with windborne seeds or seeds that survive passage through a bird's gut; reptiles that can survive for long periods stranded on a log.

In retrospect, as with most great theories, much of this seems obvious and elementary. But scientists soon began realizing that MacArthur and Wilson's work on oceanic islands applied to other areas as well, isolated patches of habitat that operated as de facto "islands." These included such discrete areas as mountaintops, caves, ponds, dunes, and habitat surrounded by development. And the ruling principles of island biogeography correlated to an uncanny degree with the results of studies of these "habitat islands." The theory has since been used to formulate conservation strategies for landscapes ranging from one-acre wetlands to vast tracts of rain forest.

In southern Arizona we have several types of habitat islands. The most grand are our cool, moist mountain ranges, known by the poetic and appropriate term *sky islands*. Surrounded by desert and other arid habitats on all sides, these ranges provide a refugia for plants such as oaks, pines, firs, and aspens, and animals such as white-tailed deer, black bears, jays, peregrine falcons, and acorn woodpeckers—species not normally associated with the lower-elevation Sonoran or Chihuahuan Deserts.

But while most of our mountain ranges are protected to at least some degree, so that the plants and smaller animals are assured a future, we now think that many of the ranges are not big enough to sustain viable populations of large mammals such as mountain lions, bighorn sheep, and black bears, unless those animals can move back and forth between the ranges, thus maintaining a healthy gene flow. Cut off, such a mountain range is akin to a small island far off the coast reached accidentally by a pair of large mammals—isolated from others of their kind, their chances of successfully colonizing the island are drastically reduced.

This is why conservation organizations are working to identify and protect what they refer to as "wildlife movement corridors" between our mountain ranges. These corridors are routes along which animals can move safely through otherwise developed or dangerous areas—possibly a wash, a heavily vegetated *bajada,* or just a region far away from houses and people. The paradigm for this new type of viable wildlife sanctuary is a series of large core reserves with corridors linking them, creating uninterrupted habitat. Done properly, these reserves and corridors can happily coexist and even intergrade with peopled and working landscapes, maintaining rural traditions and vocations while assuring a future for large mammals and wild lands. And there is a strong emotional value as well for a human visitor, who might imagine wandering for dozens or even hundreds of miles in pristine country, crossing nothing manmade except the odd road.

So: What does all this have to do with urban wildlife—besides the obvious attraction of having a city surrounded by beautiful, unspoiled nature?

In many ways, habitat within a city such as Tucson or Phoenix is a microcosm of the larger landscape. There are habitat islands large and small, and movement corridors as well. The rules of colonization and sustainable populations and species size versus territory size all apply. And everyone from city planners down to homeowners can take steps to optimize these urban habitats, maintain or forge connections between them, and enjoy the animals that flourish there.

Let's imagine a survey of typical urban habitat. Although I'll use Tucson as an example, you could do the same thing in Phoenix or any other good-sized southern Arizona town.

Those yards that retain just a single mesquite tree represent the most microscopic remnant islands of the ancestral desert. Yet in that mesquite we can expect to find one of many species of desert birds acclimated to city life: mourning or white-winged doves, cactus wrens, curve-billed thrashers, Gila woodpeckers, verdins, Lucy's warblers, and others. Now and then a Cooper's hawk might alight for a spell, watching for the small birds that are its preferred prey. Hang a bottle of sugar water on a branch and you'll be certain to attract an Anna's hummingbird, resident year-round in Arizona. Look closely at the trunk of the tree and you might spot a tree lizard *(Urosaurus ornatus)*, a native species that utilizes both native and nonnative trees, and thus has been able to persist even in heavily urbanized areas. Of course many insects and other arthropods are also apparent. Although the tree may be isolated on an otherwise barren dirt lot, it is an island of life. Just as on one of MacArthur and Wilson's remote, miniscule oceanic islands, the species found on this tree are either highly mobile or very small.

On the next block is a larger yard, with a bigger selection of native plants. There are several mesquites, an overgrown clump of prickly pear, and a Mexican palo verde (not native to the Tucson area, but a Sonoran Desert tree nonetheless). Here the birds are the same, but more numerous than in the lone tree. In the palo verde is the remnant of a verdin nest—a canta-loupe-sized globe of twigs with a nearly hidden entrance hole at the bottom. On another branch is new construction: the football-shaped nest of a pair of cactus wrens. Obviously animals are not just using this yard as a feeding or roosting station; they are living here and raising young. However modest, the yard is a living, breathing habitat.

Our next stop, still in the center of town just south of the University of Arizona, reveals a prize: a naturally vegetated wash. This one is called High School Wash, and my wife and I lived next to it for nearly a decade.

High School Wash is significantly fragmented along its original westward course to the Santa Cruz River. A section of it now runs underneath Tucson High School, through a cement culvert, so one would expect its value as a movement corridor for large mammals to be severely limited. Yet in the time we lived there, we recorded coyotes, javelina, and a single gray fox. Along most of its length, from a beginning as a ditch in the Sam Hughes neighborhood, the wash has retained a thick border of natural trees and shrubs, mixed in here and there with domestic species such as bamboo and the pernicious invader *Rhus lancea*. The bird population is astounding, with many nesting species. And reptile diversity begins to increase here, too. We have found regal horned lizards *(Phrynosoma solare)*, whiptailed lizards *(Cnemidophorus* spp.), and even blind snakes *(Leptotyphlops humilis)*—tiny, silvery, mostly subterranean snakes no larger than earthworms, with the merest dots of vestigial eyes. For a time we had a few woodrats (pack rats to you desert rats), until a neighbor poisoned them.

If we drive a bit north, we'll find one of the many older neighborhoods in midtown where the lots are very large—half an acre or more—and a lot of desert scrub survives, mixed in with the usual oleanders and eucalyptus trees. Here we can spot a couple of animals that can exist within the city limits only where there are these significant open spaces, with lots of cover in the form of both native and domestic plants. Cottontail rabbits and Gambel's quail both need more room than individual yards can provide, and they are good indicators that there is high-quality habitat in the area. In the world of island biogeography, we are now exploring those larger islands that can support more diversity. In some of these neighborhoods we might even spot a breeding colony of round-tailed ground squirrels, those hamster-sized, tan rodents that duck into holes often dug only feet from the road.

Next on the survey are the edges of urban development, where tract homes impinge on reasonably intact desert scrub. Here is where homeowners frequently report sightings of bobcats and deer, as well as encounters and problems with rattlesnakes, javelina, woodrats, and coyotes, and with arthropods such as scorpions and centipedes. This fast-growing urban edge is populated with thousands of people new to the desert, to whom many of its residents are frightening or annoying. It's a ragged, narrow band circling the city center and expanding like a blast wave, where the Tucson Fire Department is called over three thousand times every year to remove rattlesnakes and Gila monsters from areas where they had thrived for thousands of years. It's the region where urban wildlife habitat is at once at its best and most problematic.

The last stop is out in the county, where five and ten and forty-acre parcels offer their residents at least part of an experience of living within a habitat, instead of surrounding a piece of it. The larger parcels, if maintained in more or less intact condition, qualify as "real" habitat: where large mammals can move through and feed comfortably, and where a nearly complete assemblage of species still exists and breeds. Others of these rural parcels are scraped bare, refugia for derelict cars and construction materials, and probably overrun with woodrats, but otherwise sterile. Sort of the antithesis of a habitat island.

So far I've concentrated on native plant species, and with good reason. Most of our native animals evolved to eat or utilize native plants, and can be expected to do best in a familiar environment supplied with familiar resources. But animals aren't snobs. Many domestic plants are excellent for attracting or feeding native animals, and there is even evidence that lush vegetation acts as a sort of surrogate riparian area, or even sky island, for some species. For example, Aleppo pine trees and various species of eucalyptus trees (native to Australia) are the most common tall trees in southern Arizona cities. Many species of birds, up to and including raptors such as Cooper's hawks and great horned owls, nest readily in these trees; many other birds use them for roosting and cover. Likewise, many other domesticated trees and shrubs seem perfectly acceptable to lots of birds. Hummingbirds love nearly any kind of blooming plant, especially those with tubular red flowers. Even pyracantha, that overtrimmed standard of urban yards, attracts birds to its dense cover and bright-red berries. Cedar waxwings, winter visitors to Arizona, are fond of descending en masse on fruited pyracanthas and stripping them bare, as are quail and mockingbirds.

Of course there are negative issues to consider with introduced vegetation. Additional water use is a big one in a desert. Opportunistic species can also be a problem, when they escape the confines of yards and begin out-competing native plants. And giant landscaping projects such as golf courses and turfed parks do much more harm than good when they replace undis-turbed habitat, arguments from their proponents notwithstanding. But when used judiciously, nonnative landscaping can attract and benefit native ani-mals.

Urban dwellers can envy those lucky enough to live on ranches or on extensive acreage bordering public land, where deer browse, coyotes call, and nature is always close. But there's no reason the most city-bound home-owner can't create a small slice of that world, and enjoy the many species that will come to feed, rest, and breed there. A healthy little island of urban habitat can act as a connection to the bigger natural world outside the city, and as a reminder of why we must fight to protect those large wilderness preserves and movement corridors that provide the ultimate security for wildlife.

Part 1

Attracting, Feeding, and Enjoying Wildlife

Introduction
Nature, Red in Tooth and Claw

The three most basic needs of virtually all animals are food, water, and habitat (meaning a place to hide, to forage for food, or to den or nest in). By offering one or more you can turn almost any yard, in any location, into a miniature wildlife refuge.

Size is no obstacle: A patio on the back of a condo has room for a hummingbird feeder, or a potted flowering plant that will attract hummingbirds and butterflies as well. If you're lucky enough to have a big yard, so much the better. As your space goes up, so does the diversity of species you can expect to attract. Likewise, the closer your house is to relatively undisturbed habitat, the greater diversity you can expect.

But a warning is in order here: It's easy to get the wrong idea about the guests in your "wildlife refuge." To be blunt, you run the risk of disillusionment if your notion of "wildlife" ends at pretty songbirds, Bambi, and Thumper, with a few butterflies thrown in for accent.

I am an unapologetic fan of nature in all her "endless forms," as Darwin wrote. Fortunately, my wife shares this philosophy. We see no contradiction in sitting quietly on the porch, enjoying the perfectly preened scarlet of a cardinal cracking sunflower seeds at one of our feeders, then jumping up and whooping like rebels if a Cooper's hawk dives in and snags it in a cloud of feathers. We suffer no conflict when we giggle while spotlighting kangaroo rats bouncing across the desert late at night, then give thumbs up to a gopher snake with a kangaroo-rat-sized lump in its belly. The grace of the white-tailed deer that daintily browse shrubs down the hill is exceeded only by the grace and power of the resident female mountain lion that occasionally takes one down. We allow ourselves a moment of poignancy for the death, then investigate, fascinated, as the lion methodically and thoroughly consumes the carcass, and gray foxes make off with the odd leg joint.

How does one rationalize such seemingly polarized emotions? It's simple, really: Whether you believe that a divine being created the world with a snap of the fingers, or that billions of years of evolution led inexorably to the same system, or yet some reasoned fusion of the two concepts, the fact is that all natural systems operate as finely tuned, self-adjusting machines. The world has been working gloriously for hundreds of millions of years on an interdependent cycle of predator and prey, herbivore and carnivore, hunter and hunted. To pretend otherwise is folly, to resent it futile, and to attempt to change or manipulate it just downright arrogant.

Remember that everything in nature is connected—*everything*. Robinson Jeffers wrote:

> What but the wolf's tooth whittled so fine
>   The fleet limbs of the antelope?
> What but fear winged the birds, and hunger
>   Jeweled with such eyes the great goshawk's head?

A water source will attract many birds, such as this Gila woodpecker ...

Biologists know that it is the species that matters, the entire population of a kind of animal—not the individual. When a coyote kills a rabbit, it's easy to feel sorry for the rabbit—but the population of rabbits in general is much, much better off for the presence of coyotes. Take away predators, and the prey population explodes, soon exceeding its carrying capacity. And such a population is in misery, since starvation and disease are inevitably rampant. The term *balance of nature* is simplistic and misleading, since nature has always been a dynamic force, ebbing and flooding with life and death and speciation and extinction. Nevertheless, in the overall scheme of things, the balance is there.

Okay—before you decide to just forget this whole urban wildlife idea, I'm not saying that if you put out some bird seed your yard will metamorphose into some nightmarish Disney World littered with bunny corpses and circled by vultures. Millions of people around the country feed wildlife and never witness anything but the proverbial Peaceable Kingdom. I'm not even suggesting you have to *like* the idea of predators occasionally harvesting one of your feathered or furred guests. Just understand that if it does happen, it's normal, and that the predator has not only a right, but a vital purpose, to be there.

…but don't be surprised if other things show up, such as this Sonoran whipsnake. They serve a purpose too.

Besides predators, there are many species, considered "nuisances" by some people, that are also attracted to bird feeders, water sources, and yards with good cover. These range from the woodpeckers that wake us up banging on our vent pipes, to animals that can cause real safety problems, such as javelina or rattlesnakes. We'll talk about those in the next section.

1

Landscaping for Wildlife

Although most people think of feeding first when they want to attract animals, in many ways providing habitat is better. It's more permanent, less maintenance intensive, and there are few of the ancillary problems sometimes created by feeding and even watering. By planting a few trees and shrubs you provide shade, a hiding and resting place, and nesting opportunities for many species of birds. Vegetation also attracts insects, which many birds feed on. And of course the tangent benefit is that you wind up with a beautiful yard.

Virtually every animal you might expect to find in a suburban or urban yard is potential food for something else (unless you're lucky enough to have a mountain lion hanging around, which is pretty much the top of the food chain around here). So the first thing any animal looks for—before even water or food—is cover (and even the mountain lion needs cover to hunt). Instinct demands moment-to-moment survival first, sustenance next.

But you don't have to think of it as "cover," in a gritty, red-in-tooth-and-claw sense, if you'd rather not. Imagine, instead, if chef Alain Ducasse began serving his fabulous meals in a parking lot somewhere. He'd probably still attract a few clients, but not nearly as many as he does in a candlelit restaurant with linen-covered tables and fine crystal, right? So—don't think of your landscaping in terms of cover. Just call it . . . *ambiance*.

You could plant a few things haphazardly and no doubt attract many animals, but you'll have much better success, and higher species diversity (more kinds of animals), if you replicate a slice of real habitat. And to do that you need to learn a little about habitat partitioning.

Many people envision animals as being in a constant state of competition and combat over food, both with others of their kind and with other species. Actually, animals do everything they can to *avoid* competition, which wastes energy better used to find food and produce offspring. One way they do so is through habitat partitioning, or habitat layering.

If you examined a cross section of a natural habitat—say on the San Pedro River—you would find grasses and forbs (small annual and perennial plants) covering the ground, larger shrubs growing above the ground cover, then small trees growing above these, and, finally, mature cottonwood and other trees towering over all. If you recorded the bird species within this cross section, you'd find that many of them specialize in foraging in a particular layer of cover. Towhees and thrashers, for example, often hop along the ground looking for food (insects and seeds in the case of towhees; insects and berries in the case of thrashers). Above them, in shrubs, you'll typically find birds such as vireos, wrens, and many kinds of sparrows. Move higher into the trees and you'll see flycatchers, gnatcatchers, and warblers, plus the forest raptors such as Cooper's hawks and sharp-shinned hawks. Obviously, these layers aren't perfectly defined, but they are often quite evident, and help prevent competition among, for example, different species that are all insect eaters.

Habitat partitioning is apparent to a much lesser extent with mammals and reptiles, which, since most of them can't fly, are less adept at moving high in trees. Nevertheless, you'll find tree lizards in trees and whiptailed lizards on the ground, javelina rooting in the dirt while coatis forage through the branches for hackberries above them. And, of course, partitioning works in a horizontal sense as well, as some species exploit grasses and riverside habitat while others stay in the desert scrub farther from the river.

Habitat partitioning provides a good lesson for a backyard landscaper: The more diversity in your yard, the more species you're likely to attract to it.

Native Landscaping

The myth about native landscaping is that it must be scraggly, spiny, and devoid of shade. Nonsense. If you doubt this, just visit the demonstration garden at the Arizona-Sonora Desert Museum, which proves that drought-resistant landscaping can be cool and inviting as well. Okay, so it won't be some Tarzanesque jungle, or a fluffy English garden where you potter around

Saguaros show their creamy blooms in May. The blooms provide food for many desert animals, from nectar-feeding bats to doves.

in a housecoat with a trowel and watering can. But it can be inviting none-theless.

The moral reason to choose native landscaping is to conserve water. Overconsumption of ground water by a burgeoning southwestern urban population has driven some of the most tragic degradation of native habitat, especially along our former riparian corridors.

Which brings to mind a story. When I was seven, my family moved from a house in urban Tucson to a small rural development on the far northeast side. The developers had left much of the native vegetation intact—even to the extent of cutting off a limb of a mesquite tree to build our house, rather than just blading the tree—but, perversely, had planted a lush Bermuda grass lawn in our very large front yard, fed by a sprinkler system that could have extinguished the Yellowstone fires. Cottontail rabbits would feast on the grass each morning with the disbelieving frenzy of people scooping up cash spilled from an armored truck. For the first month we watered religiously (a gopher snake that lived under the front mesquite tree would crawl out and lie in the sprinkler each time, apparently savoring it). Then the water bill came, and my parents decided they really liked the idea of all-native landscaping. Later, someone from the community water co-op told us that the level in the neighborhood tank dropped by a third every time we soaked our yard. That incident gave me a lot of insight into how much water golf courses use.

So native landscaping is the responsible choice for southern Arizona homes. But as George Montgomery, the curator of botany at the Arizona-Sonora Desert Museum, says, native plants are also "without doubt the best way to attract the most native animal species."

"The animals here evolved alongside the plants, depending on them for food and shelter. So it's elementary that in your yard they'll be most attracted to what they know and can utilize best."

The key to producing an inviting and low-care native yard is planning, and much of that hinges on advance knowledge of the life cycles of the plants you intend using. Some desert plants grow very slowly, others very quickly, and others can spread out of control and turn into impenetrable tangled messes. You've seen those perfect *Sunset Magazine* yards that were photographed minutes after the landscapers left. The question is, what will those places look like in five or ten years?

A good strategy for planning a yard that will look good quickly and stay that way for a long time is to combine fast-growing trees with me-

Native landscaping attracts more native wildlife, such as this ash-throated flycatcher . . .

. . . and this curve-billed thrasher.

dium- to slow-growing shrubs, rotate annual ground cover (wildflowers, etc.), and avoid species that can get out of hand. The latter especially include certain cacti such as chollas and prickly pear, which, without careful supervision, will cover an entire yard with an impenetrable mass of spines that would make Brer Rabbit cringe. To be sure, pack rats and cactus wrens will love it, but you won't. If you want to incorporate cacti in your landscaping, stick with slow-growing, individual plants such as barrel cacti, hedgehog, and, if you've got a *lot* of time, saguaros. Many other kinds of succulents, such as agaves (which *aren't* cactus), are easy to keep in check, too.

Planning a native backyard habitat is easy if you live in a house where the builders left the natural vegetation largely or even somewhat intact. Just promote what is already there, judiciously cull what threatens to overwhelm, and add a few things for shade or ornament. It's also easy, in a twisted sort of way, if you bought in one of those developments where the earth was simply bladed bare before the builders moved in. It'll just take longer to achieve a mature landscape. And your neighbors with the winter rye grass and privet hedge will be horrified when they hear you're planning to leave some *dirt* visible. Tell them you're putting in xerophytic botanicals and chances are good they'll either call the cops on you or move.

When you shop for arid-adapted plants in local nurseries, you'll find native species as well as some that are, well, sort of native, and others that are not native at all but look the part. The best example of a sort-of-native is the Mexican palo verde *(Parkinsonea aculeata)*. While it's a true Sonoran Desert tree, it is not generally found as far north as Tucson in the wild. But it has been planted so often as an ornamental, due to its fast-growing nature and good shade, that it has colonized many areas, and even hybridized with both common local palo verde species, the foothill palo verde *(Parkinsonia microphylla)*, and blue palo verde *(Parkinsonia florida)*, according to the Desert Museum's Mark Dimmitt.

Another sort-of-native that is extremely popular as an ornamental tree is the sweet acacia *(Acacia farnesiana)*. Like the Mexican palo verde, it's common farther south in the Sonoran Desert, but does very well in Tucson and Phoenix. It grows quickly if deep-watered, produces beautiful yellow blooms in spring, and provides quite decent shade. It can be pruned into a large, multitrunked shrub or a single-trunked tree that can reach thirty feet in height and spread over a good-sized patio. It's an excellent choice.

A really striking sort-of-native is the twisted acacia *(Acacia schaffneri)*, which comes from the Chihuahuan Desert in Mexico. Its spare branches form beautiful, densely leaved shapes, although the overall shade pattern isn't dense itself. Other suitable and hardy shrubs and trees from this or nearby habitats you might consider include palo blanco *(Acacia willardiana)*, Wright acacia *(Acacia wrightii)*, palo brea *(Parkinsonia praecox)*, condalia *(Condalia globosa)*, coursetia *(Coursetia microphylla)*, and Gregg ash *(Fraxinus greggii)*.

Many authentic local native trees and shrubs are well suited to the domestic life. Whitethorn acacia *(Acacia constricta)* attains sort of huge-shrub size, as does catclaw acacia *(Acacia greggii)*. The Sonoran Desert's signature tree (one of them at least), velvet mesquite *(Prosopis velutina)*, acts, well, right at home here, although it's slow growing by ornamental standards. But it can be pruned into a large and stately shape. Blue palo verde *(Parkinsonia florida)*, which puts on those breathtaking displays of yellow flowers in April, makes a wonderful yard tree, as does foothill palo verde *(Parkinsonia microphylla)*, a favored nest tree for verdins and mourning doves. More subtle in bloom, but just as lovely, is desert willow *(Chilopsis linearis)*.

For smaller native shrubs, consider desert honeysuckle *(Anisacanthus thurberi)*, the hardy (but fast spreading—watch it) fourwing saltbush *(Atriplex canescens)*, brittlebush *(Encelia farinosa)*, and indigo bush *(Dalea pulchra)*. Fairy duster *(Calliandra eriophylla)* will grace you with delicate pink flowers . . . in December! If you look closely, you'll see that it's actually the flower's long stamens that give it the color.

George Montgomery also suggests planting a few native bunch grasses, such as sideoats grama, which provide nice ground cover and natural seed for birds.

For more information about native landscaping, buy Judy Mielke's excellent book *Native Plants for Southwestern Landscapes*. Also very useful are the booklets published by the Arizona Native Plant Society.

Nonnative Plants

I probably shouldn't be telling you this. But the fact is that, issues of water use aside, many nonnative plants are great for attracting animals you might not otherwise see within the city limits. Years ago we lived in a university-

Butterflies and Butterfly Gardens

Butterflies and flowers were made for each other ... literally. Although little is known directly about butterfly origins because of their cryptic presence in the fossil record (soft-bodied organisms don't fossilize well), scientists are pretty sure that flowering plants and butterflies evolved concurrently during the Cretaceous period, 135 million to 65 million years ago. Today, they are inextricably linked: Butterflies rely on nectar for food, and many flowers rely entirely on butterflies for pollination. It's just a happy side effect for us that butterflies are so beautiful. They're also as mobile as birds, and thus as accessible to any inner-city resident with a lantana or rosemary plant.

There are about as many butterfly species in Arizona as there are bird species—over 325. Richard Bailowitz and James Brock, in their superb book *Butterflies of Southeastern Arizona,* list over 240 species just in our corner of the state. And while butterflies peak in numbers in summer, you can see them at any time of year when the air temperature is above fifty degrees or so (Bailowitz and Brock have recorded forty-six species active in January). Our species range in size from glorious two-tailed swallowtails and giant swallowtails down to tiny but dapper blues and skippers. Royalty is represented by monarchs, queens, and empresses. Colors vary from sulphurous yellow and luminescent blue to a velvety black deeper than the background of an Elvis painting. In November, millions of snout butterflies feed on the snowdrift-like blooms of desert broom, and several species visit the pink flowers of fairy dusters and other winter bloomers. In spring and summer, the population really explodes.

Adult butterflies commonly feed on the nectar of blooms of several different species, but many of their caterpillars have evolved to feed on the leaves of just one species. The pipevine swallowtail, a handsome, blue-black butterfly, produces a caterpillar (sounds so much better than *larva,* doesn't it?) that feeds exclusively on a small desert vine called a pipevine. The pipevine produces a toxin that the caterpillar incorporates into its own tissues, making it distasteful to most predators. Many other butterfly species pursue a similar strategy. Gardeners have historically panicked at the first sign of caterpillar activity, but they rarely do significant damage in a yard with a diverse mix of plants (artificial monocultures, such as on commercial farms, can be a different story).

The Western National Parks Association book *50 Common Butterflies of the Southwest* is a good place to start learning butterflies, but I highly

Native plants such as this *Gutierrezia* attract lots of butterflies.

recommend you move on to *Butterflies of Southeastern Arizona*, a much more complete book. Its only downside for the novice is that the authors use Latin names a lot—but that's okay. You'll bewilder your friends immensely someday by suddenly crying, "Oh my God, look at that gorgeous *Nymphalis antiopa*." And while it does seem a shame to have mostly black and white photos in a butterfly book, there are ninety color plates in the back, illuminating some of our most common species. Possibly even better, at least as far as illustrations go, is *Butterflies of Arizona, a Photographic Guide*, by Bob Stewart and Hank and Priscilla Brodkin.

When planning your backyard habitat, don't forget to provide for butterflies. They are attracted to almost all blooming plants, but shrubs with yellow flowers seem to work especially well. Appendix 1 has a list of good butterfly plants.

area house with several pyracantha shrubs growing up the front wall. One day, when a full crop of bright-red berries was quite in evidence, we heard some unusual bird noises, and discovered a large flock of cedar waxwings gorging on the fruit. They stayed for several hours before disappearing as quickly as they had come.

Many other nonnative plants fill vegetation niches that otherwise wouldn't exist here. In essence, there might be a sort of sky island effect going on, where these artificially lush pockets provide a refuge for species that would ordinarily pass up the place.

Before someone takes this and runs with it in the wrong direction, note that this is emphatically not an endorsement of metastasizing golf courses on the city edge. Such artificial landscapes permanently destroy natural desert habitat, vastly reducing both plant and animal diversity. The deer and rabbits seen by golfers are but a tiny fraction of the original breadth of inhabitants.

Other nonnative plants can be much worse than mere water wasters. Invasive and opportunistic species such as African sumac, buffel grass, fountain grass, Lehman's lovegrass, and tamarisk trees can replace native vegetation and disrupt entire ecosystems, as tamarisk has done along many southwestern rivers, and Lehman's has over thousands of acres of desert grassland. Those lovely fires we see each 4th of July under the fireworks display on A Mountain in Tucson? They're fueled by buffel grass, which was planted by the state highway department along many roads and has been spreading into the desert scrub. Buffel-fed fires kill cactus and other plants not adapted to a fire regime. The buffel grass just grows right back, stronger than ever. Ask the salespeople at your nursery about invasive species and which ones to avoid. If they give you a blank look, leave and find another nursery.

Attracting and Feeding Birds
(and Other Winged Creatures)

The joy one feels watching a bird forage outside the kitchen window, or hearing it sing from a tree in the backyard, is a nearly universal human emotion. For many people, this joy extends to watching other animals as well—mammals, insects (well, at least butterflies), and even reptiles and amphibians. But birds seem to exert a particular hold on us.

It's not hard to figure why. First, they are beautiful in both texture and color, flashing across our sight in hues subtle or brilliant, leaving us the occasional gift of a discarded azure or red or earth-toned feather, which we pick up and stroke across the inside of our wrist to feel its softness. Second, birds are accessible. There is no concreted alley in any city that birds cannot find if a bit of greenery and some water or food is on offer.

But above these details, it must be their wings that captivate us. For, barring some as-yet-unimagined feat of bioengineering, the only way humans will ever fly is with the help of snarling machines, a rude and stinking contrast to the graceful levitation of the lowliest street pigeon. Nothing surpasses the awe with which we view this ultimate symbol of freedom—just look at the way we incorporate it into the images of our most mythical beings: fairies, angels, superheroes, and gods.

Over 350 species of birds have been recorded in southern Arizona—half of all the species found in the entire United States. There are two main reasons for this astonishing abundance. One is the diversity of habitats to be found here, from the low deserts to grasslands to oak woodlands to pine and fir forests on the tops of our sky islands. Thus we boast both roadrunners and peregrine falcons, cactus wrens and red-faced warblers, Gambel's quail and Steller's jays—birds of widely varying habits that exist within just a few miles of each other. The other factor is two southern Arizona rivers, the San Pedro and the Santa Cruz, which are vital pathways for migrating birds.

Each spring a staggering five billion birds fly north from wintering grounds in Mexico, Central, and South America, to nest and rear their young in the temperate latitudes of the United States and Canada, where productivity of seeds and insects peaks during the long days of summer. Most migrating birds fly at night and rest and feed during the day, and it makes sense that they would do so along north-south oriented corridors where food and water are reliably available. In the Southwest, they frequently use mountain ranges, which, because of our basin and range topography, tend to be oriented north-south, or they use the rivers, where the extra density of riparian vegetation equals extra productivity of food, cover, and, of course, water. In fall, on their way south again to escape dropping temperatures and shorter days, they use the same routes.

But not all the migrating birds stay strictly within narrow corridors; they often show up in urban backyards as well. Migration adds a lot of variety to backyard bird-watching during March and April, and again in August and September.

In addition, southern Arizona is a terminus for migration of many species, some of which fly north and spend the summer here (such as many warblers, orioles, and tanagers), others of which fly south to our area for the winter (such as white-crowned sparrows and northern harriers). And, of course, there are dozens of resident species, here year-round. The result is that there is always something interesting happening birdwise in southern Arizona. In fact, southeastern Arizona is repeatedly listed as one of the top two or three birding areas in the United States.

Backyard Bird-Watching

There are bird-watchers, and then there are Birders.

On one hand is the bird-watcher with whom, in a recent poll, over 70 percent of Americans included themselves: You see a pretty bird in the backyard, you stop what you're doing and, well, watch it. Species? Who knows? Pretty, though, isn't it?

On the other hand is the Birder. This is the individual with the thirteen-hundred-dollar Swarovski EL binoculars suspended more or less permanently around his or her neck, a *Sibley* or *National Geographic* bird guide (rarely needed) in a special belt pouch, power-walking shoes, and pastel-colored ripstop clothes with sleeves and legs that zip off. The Birder can differentiate female hummingbirds from fifty yards off and talk longer than a Fidel Castro speech on lower beak color in *Empidonax* flycatchers. He or she is looking to add species number 683 to the North American list, and has already booked a return trip to the Pribilof Islands for next summer. The Birder often uses the phrase "Oh, that's *just* a (fill in species)" when an unwashed dilettante asks the identity of some plebeian bird.

I fall happily between these two extremes. Yes, I have an excellent pair of binoculars, and I've even taught bird-watching for beginners. But I still refer frequently to my field guide, and quite often pretend I don't see those flycatchers in the genus *Empidonax,* to avoid having to wring out of my brain the microscopic differences between the species. Plus, I still get as big a kick out of watching such utterly pedestrian birds as black-throated sparrows and Cassin's kingbirds as I do adding a new species to my list. List? Actually, I don't keep one. Oh, occasionally I'll do a specific one, such as a "yard list" or a "birds I saw in Namibia list," but overall I'm just not aroused by the concept of counting how many species I've ever seen. And I've met too many Birders to whom "getting" that next bird becomes the overriding factor—even if it means harassing the bird in question to do so, such as using alarm calls to lure it off a nest so it can be seen and checked off.

Before you get the idea I think all listers are evil, let me mention my friend Will Russell, who founded Wings, one of the biggest and most respected bird-watching tour companies in the world. Will, who is surely among the four or five best Birders on the planet, is as happy sitting for hours on our porch watching Gambel's quail and cactus wrens as he is leading a group looking for a rare five-striped sparrow. And I know dozens of other people with world-class lists who haven't lost their sense of wonder. So it's not always a terminal affliction.

It's easy to make fun of the fanatic listers (in England, they're known as Twitchers). But don't let caricatures discourage you from trying a bit of backyard bird-watching. It's not only fun—done right, it's a fantastic do-it-yourself course in natural history.

Looking at colors and size and markings is only part of what's involved in identifying a bird. There's also a big portion of behavior and biology intrinsic to the process. A good Birder doesn't just see what a bird looks like, he sees what it's doing, where it is, when it's there, what noises it is making, and a dozen other details. Once you start noticing the same things about the same birds for the fourth or fifth time, you realize you're learning about the *life* of that bird, not just its appearance. And pretty soon an interesting thing happens: You'll find yourself able to identify certain birds by what they're doing, even if you're too far away to make out field markings. Birders call this *jizz*. You pick out the curve-billed thrasher under a shrub by the way it's flinging debris aside as it digs for insects; a Gila woodpecker by how it hops up a vertical trunk; a kingbird by how it dives on a passing hawk.

The best way to start identifying birds is to buy a very simple guide, such as the Western National Parks Association's *Fifty Common Birds of the Southwest*. It's perfect for familiarizing yourself with the species you're most likely to see in southern Arizona, in habitats from desert to mountain to lake.

But if you pay attention, you'll soon see birds in the yard that don't match any of the book's photographs. At this point one of two things will happen. You'll shrug and think, *oh well,* and ignore it, or you'll think, *Gee, that looks sort of like a Scott's oriole, but not quite. Maybe I need a better book.*

If it's the latter, you're toast. Pretty soon you'll be saying things to your friends like "*No,* a thousand dollars isn't a lot to spend on binoculars when you consider they'll last me the rest of my life." An absolutely true statement, by the way.

The one vital point to remember about birding is not to get frustrated. You'll *never* be able to identify every bird you see, unless you become Will Russell. The fun is in the trying, and in succeeding more and more often as you go.

The very best way to become adept at identifying new birds is to learn the characteristics of different families, so you can eliminate possibilities quicker. Once you know the general shape and behavior of sparrows, or warblers, or flycatchers, it helps you to zero in on the right section in your field guide, which saves a lot of page flipping.

A good place to practice birding is in the walk-in aviary at the Desert Museum, where you won't even need binoculars. Or take a beginning birding class offered by the Tucson or Phoenix Audubon Society.

Hummingbirds

An adult broad-tailed hummingbird has a resting pulse rate of about six hundred beats per minute—ten heartbeats every second. That can double when the bird is engaged in a vigorous courtship display. Round it to a million beats every day. This furious pace is supported by a metabolism which, if enlarged to human proportions, would require 150,000 calories a day to fuel—the equivalent of twenty-five chocolate cakes. So it's no wonder hummingbirds battle so ferociously over our sugar-water feeders, which provide them with an excellent source of energy-rich carbohydrates.

Contrary to what many people still believe, however, hummingbirds cannot subsist solely on sugar water and flower nectar. They are, in fact, voracious insectivores as well, gleaning small insects around the same flowers from which they gather nectar, or perching in trees and darting out to snag gnats and mosquitoes on the wing (a remarkable feat of dexterity considering the configuration of their beaks; try to grab a fly out of mid-air with chopsticks sometime—it's a *lot* harder than the Karate Kid made it look). These insects provide vital proteins and other nutrients; a captive hummer fed only sugar water would quickly starve to death.

Despite their turbocharged existence, hummingbirds are remarkably long-lived. Although the average life span in the wild is three to four years, one bird banded by hummingbird researcher Bill Calder survived to twelve, and captive hummers have surpassed even that. I did the math: Even if such a Methuselah were a veritable couch potato (twig potato?) by hummingbird standards, its tiny heart still beat over four billion times during its life—four thousand million beats of a pump the size of a fat grain of rice.

Hummingbirds are found only in the Western Hemisphere, and there, mostly in the tropics. Arizona rightly boasts of hosting more hummer species than any other state except Texas—seventeen have been recorded here, although a couple of those are *extremely* rare (such as the single sighting of a bumblebee hummingbird—in 1896!). That number pales in comparison to over 330 found in Central and South America. Still, we are blessed with our dozen-plus, several of which happily feed and breed in the middle of town.

If you're lucky, a hummingbird might build its wristwatch-sized nest in your yard.

Feeding Hummingbirds

Not only are hummingbirds among the most lovely and fascinating birds to watch, they are also among the easiest to attract. You don't have to buy fancy and expensive hummingbird food preparations; a simple mixture of one part white sugar to four parts water is an excellent augmentation to the birds' natural diet. I have always brought the mixture to a boil to sterilize it, but Karen Krebbs, a conservation biologist at the Desert Museum, says this isn't necessary as long as you change the food every week in the winter and twice a week in the summer to prevent fermentation. As a homeowner attracting wild birds, you won't have the stringent dietary concerns of the museum, whose captive hummingbirds must be fed a rigorously researched concoction that provides all their needs. Your hummingbirds will get all the protein, vitamins, and other nutrients they require from the insects they catch and nectar they consume from flowers. Incidentally, the four-to-one water to sugar ratio more or less duplicates the sucrose level in the nectar of the flowers most attractive to hummingbirds. Some hummingbird experts suggest reducing the ratio to five-to-one in hot weather, when the birds need more water than sucrose. Never substitute honey, which can promote a fungus fatal to the birds.

A few myths have floated around concerning other supposed dangers involved in feeding hummingbirds. Chief among these is the assertion that, with a food source nearby, the birds will not migrate to escape cold weather in the fall, and will then succumb to the first freeze. Those who ascribe to this theory say you should stop putting out food at the end of summer. But they are wrong. First, bird migration is triggered by photoperiod (the length of the day) and other factors, more than the availability of food. In fact, hummingbirds and other migratory species generally migrate while food *is* still plentiful, since they need to gorge to store energy for the exhausting flight south.

Furthermore, at least one hummingbird common in Arizona cities, the Anna's, is a year-round resident, and sometimes begins *nesting* in December. Costa's hummingbirds, often found in suburbs, can begin nesting in January. And several other species sometimes overwinter in southern Arizona. So there are actually excellent reasons to maintain a hummingbird feeder all year.

Shopping for a hummingbird feeder can be bewildering. There are dozens of styles, each of which is touted as the best available. Is there really any difference in performance? The answer is absolutely, although personal preference plays a part as well.

First, of course, the feeder must attract hummingbirds. But that's not hard—any splash of red is sufficient for that task, and once the birds learn the location of the feeder even that is not necessary. More important is how easy the feeder is to clean.

If you commit to offering food to hummingbirds, you must also commit to being fanatic about keeping the feeder clean. No exceptions or slacking off allowed. The feeder should be washed out with a mild bleach solution (a half ounce or one tablespoon bleach per quart of water) every week during summer, every two weeks in winter, to prevent fermentation of the

Just occasionally, hummingbirds will share.

food mixture or the growth of algae, both of which can be harmful to the birds. So look for a feeder that is easy to disassemble and clean, with no constricted filler openings through which you cannot at least get a bottle brush.

Another concern is dripping. If you're going to hang the feeder on a patio or other place where you walk, you don't want sugar water dripping, splashing, and making a gooey mess under the feeder. Feeders with pendant tubes tend to drip more than saucer-shaped feeders or other styles with the feeding ports on top.

Capacity is an additional factor. If you live in the middle of town, where you might expect to have fewer than a half-dozen birds around, a feeder that holds a pint or less will be sufficient. But near the edge of town, especially near the foothills, your feeder will attract hordes of hummers, and you might find yourself refilling it twice a day. Either buy a larger feeder or add extra feeders in different locations.

My personal favorite style of hummingbird feeder is the flat, saucer, or pan style (such as one called the HummZinger) with a perching ring. They're drip free, a cinch to clean, and come in different sizes to suit particular needs. Many of them also incorporate a depression on the top, surrounding the hanging rod, which can be filled with water or, better, Vaseline, to discourage ants from climbing down the rod and getting into the food. If your feeder isn't so equipped, you can buy a separate little cupped gizmo called an ant guard, which hangs between the feeder and the tree.

Hummingbirds will find and use a feeder no matter where you put it, but a few guidelines will hasten and maximize your success. Hang the feeder where there is plenty of flying room around it, but also where resting perches are nearby. If possible, keep it in the sun when it's cold, and in the shade during summer. Trees are obviously a good choice, but so are the eaves of your house, on a porch or in front of a window, which allows you to watch the birds more closely.

Hummingbirds defend feeders fiercely against other hummers and even other species. Don't worry about it; it's just what they do, and all part of the show. If you find that one hummingbird is dominating your feeder, the easiest solution is to put up more feeders. Then you get to watch *several* hummingbirds dominating feeders. Seriously, hanging multiple feeders is the best way to increase the hummer population around your house. Try to put them out of sight of each other, so one bird doesn't attempt to defend them all (believe me, it happens). Along these lines, Dan True, in his

During migration in spring and late summer, competition at hummingbird feeders becomes fierce. There are eight here vying for space.

wonderful book *Hummingbirds of North America, Attracting, Feeding, and Photographing,* believes that feeders with deep, fake flowers at the feeding ports are not as attractive to hummingbirds, since it's more difficult for them to keep an eye out for competitors or predators while feeding. Makes sense to me.

You'll probably notice a significant increase in hummingbird activity in March and April, and again in August and September. This is when thousands of migrating birds move through, temporarily spiking local populations.

Another good way to increase hummingbird activity is to put out some old fruit, such as bananas or peaches, which will attract fruit flies that the birds love. But don't put it too close to the feeder, because the flies produced by the fruit will get inside and drown by the score.

One of the best ways to attract hummingbirds is by incorporating plants they can feed from in your landscaping. Many flowers have evolved specifically to attract hummingbirds. Typically they have red, tubular flowers, which are suited to the hummingbird's long beak and which maximize transfer of pollen to the bird—the only reason the plant is trying to attract it in the first place. Appendix 2 has a list of good hummingbird plants.

Other Guests at Feeders

Bees can be a problem on hummingbird feeders, and they're much harder to dissuade than ants. I've yet to see a truly bee-proof feeder, although some are better than others (in the HummZinger saucer-style feeder, the sugar water level can be kept low enough that it's difficult for bees and wasps to feed). But there are a couple of other ways of dealing with bees.

First, buy a feeder without yellow flowers on the feeding ports. Biologists have known for years that red attracts hummingbirds while yellow is more attractive to bees, but many feeder makers still insist on those yellow flowers.

Still, no matter what color those flowers, bees will find them. Some feeders are available with bee guards, little plastic cages that fit over the feeder's ports. While these might keep bees from feeding directly from the source, there always seems to be enough spillage and slop of sugar water from feeding birds to coat the guard itself, and the area around it, so the bees still cluster on it. Not very effective.

A better strategy is to provide them with their own source of sugar water. Try sitting near the feeder for a time, and see if you can determine from which direction the bees are flying to the feeder (it's often surprisingly easy). Placing an open, shallow pan of sugar water somewhere along this line will detour a lot of bees. Since the flowers bees normally utilize have a higher concentration of sucrose than most hummingbird flowers, try using a three to one water-sugar mixture to make the decoy even more attractive. But even plain water works to some extent, as bees are after moisture as well as sugar when they raid feeders.

Another method sounds like an urban legend, but I've tested it and seen it work. Avon Skin-So-Soft oil, painted around (but not directly in!) the feeding ports with a small artist's brush, is amazingly effective at deterring both bees and wasps. Its only real disadvantage is that it's rather volatile, meaning it evaporates quickly in hot weather. Sometimes reapplication is needed every few hours to maintain effectiveness. But it does work. I've also heard that a product called Off Skintastic does the job. Be cautious if you use such products, since they would be extremely harmful to the birds if ingested or smeared in their feathers.

By the way, as a *general rule* (meaning I accept absolutely no responsibility if your results differ), bees—even Africanized bees—are *generally* quite unaggressive around feeders or water sources. Their defensive instincts peak at or near the hive, so you can approach and even shake bees off feeders with little risk of being stung, unless one flies off the wrong way and gets stuck in your hair or clothing, at which point it might sting defensively.

Wasps are generally similar, but I have heard of a few people being stung by wasps near feeders, so perhaps more caution is advised. They certainly discourage hummingbirds. If you have a real problem with the paper wasps that are common in southern Arizona in the summer, you can buy a wasp trap and hang it near your feeders. They work well to at least diminish the population. But use circumspection—wasps have a niche, too.

Dan True claims that if you use a household vacuum to remove a few bees or wasps when they first start showing up, it will keep others away for days or even weeks. I haven't tried it, but it's worth the experiment. Incidentally, Dan also offers plans for making your own ant guard from a Vienna Sausage tin. But he doesn't say what you're supposed to do with those slippery little sausage-like things first.

Several other kinds of birds also visit hummingbird feeders. Gila woodpeckers are helpless sugar junkies, and coincidentally well adapted to access the food, with their long tongues designed for getting insects out of holes. Verdins try their best to suck out a few drops, although they lack the equipment to be really effective. And occasionally finches and other species will have a go.

People often ask how to keep Gila woodpeckers away from their hummingbird feeders, to which my reply is "Why?" I enjoy watching other birds at my hummingbird feeders, and I've never had the slightest impression that they cause the hummingbirds more than minor annoyance. But if you want to have one feeder that is woodpecker proof, buy a bottle style with the tube coming out the bottom. If woodpeckers can't land on the feeder they can't get to the food.

Nectar-Feeding Bats

In outlying areas of town, especially near the foothills, you might discover some summer morning that your hummingbird feeder, which you swear was three-quarters full the night before, is now bone dry. If you're lucky enough to find yourself in this situation, it means you have nectar-feeding bats visiting your feeder.

Nectar-feeding bats sometimes visit hummingbird feeders during the warm months.

There are twenty-eight species of bats in Arizona, but only two—the Mexican long-tongued *(Choeronycteris mexicana)*, and the lesser long-nosed *(Leptonycteris curasoae)*—have evolved to feed on the nectar, pollen, and some fruits of such plants as agaves, saguaros, and organ-pipe cacti. They have elongated snouts that perform the same function as the hummingbird's beak. Both species migrate north from Mexico into southern Arizona, following the blooming cycle of their food plants (columnar cacti on the way north, agaves on the way south later in the season); thus they are here only in summer (although there have been a few reports of overwintering individuals). Of the two, the long-tongued is thought to be more common—in fact, the long-nosed bat is an endangered species, although it seems to be recovering and might even be de-listed at some point. Both these bats provide a vital pollinating service to several Sonoran Desert cacti and succulents. In one study by bat biologist Donna Howell, successful seed production in agaves fell to a fraction of normal when bats were excluded from the flowers.

For several years, my wife and I lived on a remote U.S. Fish and Wildlife Service property in Brown Canyon, underneath Baboquivari Peak about fifty miles southwest of Tucson. Our hummingbird feeders there attracted a constant stream of bats on summer nights. By shining a red light on one of the feeders (most mammals don't see red well) and moving slowly, we could get within a couple of feet of the feeder and watch, entranced, as the bats swooped in, fluttered in a sort of jive-hover for a second at most, and grabbed a few tonguefuls of sugar water. They seemed to come in along a well-defined flight path designed to reduce congestion, like fighter planes coming in for refueling. At other times, we'd just sit in the dark, with the bats barely outlined against the moonlight, listening to the soft flutter of their wings.

Rather incredibly (to me, anyway), there are people who consider bats at hummingbird feeders a problem. If you are one of them, take your feeders in at night. Problem solved.

I *have* been asked by several people who enjoy having bats around if rabies is a concern when one handles the feeder to refill or clean it. Several bat experts I talked to said no. First, rabies occurrence in bats is no higher than in any other group of mammals, despite folklore (see more about this in the next chapter's section on bats). More important, the rabies virus dies quickly when exposed to open air and especially to sunlight. The chances of transmission of a viable virus from bat to feeder and into your bloodstream are remote. You're probably more likely to be vaporized by a stray meteor just as you're reaching up to unhook the feeder: "*Hey,* what's tha—"

Feeding Seed-Eating Birds

On the surface, this seems like a *real* simple project:

1. Buy birdseed.
2. Spread birdseed on ground.
3. Watch birds eat seed.

Indeed, there is much to recommend this approach. It's cheap, and you get to watch birds hopping around on the ground and foraging like they do naturally. Also, there is some evidence that spreading seed widely might reduce transmission of trichomoniasis (see sidebar, page 40). The theory is that a seed picked up by an infected bird, then dropped because it couldn't swallow it, has a better chance of drying out—thus killing the protozoan pathogen—before another bird finds it.

Many species of birds, such as this mourning dove, are happy to eat seed spread on the ground.

But there are downsides to ground feeding, too. Seed on the ground is highly likely to attract animals other than the ones you're looking for. Javelina love it, as do rock squirrels. Many other rodents devour birdseed nearly as efficiently. And if it rains and the seed gets damp, it might harbor pathogens longer (it won't, however, sprout and fill your yard with unwanted weeds—commercial birdseed is irradiated to render it inviable).

The simple solution to these problems is to put the seed in a feeder of some sort, on a post or hung in a tree. The side benefit—and the reason most people buy feeders to start with—is that you can position it where it's easiest for you to watch your avian guests.

It seems there's always a market for complicating simplicity. Walk into a bird supply store and look around at the approximately three thousand varieties of seed feeders on offer, and you might think you've found the ultimate expression of this axiom. There are wooden feeders, metal feeders, and plastic feeders, round feeders, square feeders, squirrel-proof feeders, bird-proof feeders (really! more on this later), and feeders shaped like barns, outhouses, log cabins, and various government buildings in Washington, D.C.

Such diversions are almost exclusively for our own amusement—I have to doubt whether a finch cares if it's eating out of a coffee can with holes punched in the side or a replica of the White House—but they do no harm as long as the basic design of the feeder is sound.

Most seed feeders are designed to use the inexpensive scratch mix sold everywhere, a mixture of milo, millet, cracked corn, and other seeds, with a bit of sunflower seed thrown in. But research has shown that the seed preferred by most birds is black oil sunflower seed, followed by white proso millet. Striped sunflower seed is also good. So look for a mix that has a high percentage of these seeds. Even if it costs a little more, your success will be much greater. And since many birds simply reject much of the filler in cheap scratch mix, the actual difference in cost might not be great at all, since you can use less of the better seed.

Look for a feeder that protects the seed from rain, and that holds enough so you won't have to refill it twice a day. Plastic feeders are susceptible to ultraviolet deterioration if placed in direct sunlight, and wood will dry out and weather if not maintained. Otherwise, the style is pretty much up to you.

Ideally, a seed feeder should be mounted in the open, but not too far from a tree or other cover. This helps prevent predators such as neighborhood cats from stalking too close, but gives the birds a place to escape and roost. Mounting the feeder on a metal post keeps unwanted small mammals from getting into it.

If you're lucky, your feeder will attract a nicely balanced mix of species. But sometimes you'll find it dominated by finches and sparrows, or doves, or even street pigeons ("air roaches," as some of us refer to them). This doesn't bother some people, but it can get expensive feeding hordes of doves and sparrows, and besides, it's nice to see other kinds of birds once in a while. An exclusionary feeder is what you need.

Some tube-style seed feeders are made with a wire grid surrounding the central tube, with holes small enough to exclude larger birds. These are effective at keeping out doves and pigeons, although English sparrows and finches can get in. Some platform feeders are also equipped with exclusionary tops.

Another feeder we found is designed to offer cardinals and their relatives, pyrrhuloxias, an exclusive food source. Both birds love pure black oil sunflower seed, which is more expensive than any mix. The feeder we bought was made with a clever, counterweighted perch and a sliding cover

Cardinal feeders keep most other birds out—except those that weigh close to the same, such as this black-headed grosbeak. But it's just as handsome anyway.

over the port where the bird feeds. The counterweight is set to the average weight of a cardinal—a lighter finch or sparrow won't depress it enough, and a dove will depress it too much. It takes a while for the cardinal to learn to perch on the bar and wait for the cover to slide open, but once they get the hang of it they enjoy their own exclusive food source. My wife loves to point out that the female of our resident cardinal pair figured out the mechanism days before her mate, who would sit on the roof of the feeder and watch her as she ate. I think he was just being a gentleman. Janice Bowers, the botanist and natural history writer, told me that house finches learned to sit side by side on her cardinal feeder's perch, and that Gila woodpeckers grip the side of the feeder with one foot and *push down* on the perch with the other to access the seed. Amazing! Nevertheless, this design is still very effective at excluding most other birds.

Lesser goldfinches are beautiful little part-yellow birds that reside year-round in southern Arizona. They eat small seed from weeds and thistles, and love commercially available thistle seed (properly called *niger*). You can attract them with an inexpensive feeder that is nothing but a socklike tube of fine mesh fabric. When filled with seed, the birds can hang on the fabric and pull the seeds though the mesh. Many other species can't access this seed. Even better is a clear plastic tube thistle feeder with tiny feeding ports *underneath* the perches, since goldfinches frequently forage upside down for seeds inside pendant flowers. Not many other birds can perform the trick effectively.

Other Good Bird Foods

Got an orange, apple, or other fruit that's a bit too ripe? Cut it in half and set it out on a wall or branch or, better, impale it on a nail driven into a tree limb or fence post. Birds love the sweetness and moisture. Many birds also go crazy for peanut butter, and you can buy a special feeder made with a coarse screen in front of a board, designed so you can smear a good deal of peanut butter on it.

If you're lucky enough to have wrens (cactus wrens, rock wrens, canyon wrens, it doesn't matter) at your house and you're not too squeamish, buy a container of live mealworms from a pet store, and one of those small, clear plastic tray feeders that attach to a window with suction cups. Once the wrens discover it they'll stop by regularly to see if it's been replenished.

This Bewick's wren
nested in an old Coke
machine.

Don't put more than three or four mealworms in at a time—that's plenty
to attract the birds, without costing you too much.

Incidentally, wrens are vastly entertaining to have around. They explore
the most twisted and hazardous-looking cracks and crannies looking for
insects. Several years ago, a canyon wren made its way down our chimney
one day, and was stunned to discover an entire new world to investigate, a
sort of wren Pellucidar. It would visit nearly daily, hopping across the desk
where I sat writing with barely a glance at me, foraging behind all our
books and appliances, and pooping on the furniture. One day a cacophony
of wren indignation erupted in the bathroom. We went in and found the
bird perched on the medicine cabinet looking in the mirror, stridently demanding to know who this (admittedly handsome) intruder was.

A canyon wren raised two successive broods in this flowerpot on our porch.

Bird feeder raid: A Mexican opossum makes off with some fruit from a platform in Brown Canyon.

Suet, available at wild bird stores and at some butcher shops, is excellent food for many birds, especially insect eaters. Overwintering birds can use the extra energy provided by the pure fat of suet. Suet feeders are simple wire cages into which pieces of suet can be dropped. Prepared suet cakes fit exactly, and contain other goodies such as peanut butter and seed to add flavor and nutrients.

Birdhouses

Building birdhouses is one of those crafts that children just don't do anymore—adults either, for that matter. And what a shame. There are few things more richly satisfying than watching a bird choose something you have built to use as its home and carrying nesting materials to it, and, weeks later, seeing fledglings clinging to the opening while their parents entice them to fly.

One of the problems with your generic homebuilt birdhouse, however, is that birds tend to be extremely picky about the sizes of their houses, where they are placed, and even of the placement and size of the entrance hole. This isn't just snobbery—it is a survival imperative. The way birds locate and build their natural houses has evolved over millennia to give them the best chance of successfully raising their young, in terms of weather exposure, inside temperature, and resistance to predators and nest para-

Kestrels often use
nest boxes.

sites (other birds that lay eggs in the nest, to be reared unknowingly by the surrogate parents). For an artificial birdhouse to be accepted by a bird, it must closely replicate these parameters.

So if you'd like to try offering housing for birds, it's probably best to begin with a commercially made model suited to those species you know live near you, and which are known to utilize birdhouses. Or you can build your own with plans suited to those species. I did a web search and found numerous sites with such information.

In southern Arizona, birds known to use birdhouses include kestrels, screech and elf owls, northern flickers, Bewick's and house wrens, house finches and English sparrows, and purple martins.

Water for Birds

When I was growing up, our yard always sported one of those classic cement birdbaths with the statue of St. Francis in the middle. Actually, it was a very well-designed product, with a shallow pan that sloped gradually deeper toward the center, where St. Francis gazed down benignly, his head always lightly encrusted with bird poop. It was easy for birds of any size to immerse themselves comfortably, with no chance of getting stuck or submerged.

Many similar products (with or without the saint) are still around, and they make excellent waterers. Their chief disadvantage is that the water in the shallow pan evaporates quickly, necessitating frequent refilling. But this is a blessing in disguise, since it gives you the opportunity to flush out and clean the bath to prevent algae buildup. Occasional scrubbing with a brush and mild bleach solution (a couple tablespoons bleach to a quart of water, then well rinsed) might be necessary.

About a zillion other types of receptacles can be pressed into service for either bathing or watering birds, of course, from old hubcaps to expensive copper fountains. Just make sure the birds can safely drink or bathe without risk of falling into deep water. Some pottery birdbaths I've seen lack a shallow part; a flat rock placed in the middle will provide a safe perch.

Standing water does introduce a potential problem however, when contagious diseases are present in the local bird population (see sidebar). A possible solution is running water, which can actually be provided with very little waste.

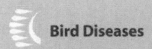 **Bird Diseases**

As we have learned more about avian biology, we have learned more about avian diseases, some of which are easily spread by practices used by homeowners who feed and water birds.

One of the most common of these diseases is trichomoniasis, which is caused by a protozoan, *Trichomonas gallinae*. Trichomoniasis is most often found in birds in the dove family, including pigeons. However, it can also spread to other birds, such as quail and finches. Raptors such as hawks and falcons also contract it, by feeding on infected prey (among falconers the disease is known as *frounce*)—in fact, a study on nesting Cooper's hawks in Tucson revealed significant fledgling mortality due to trichomoniasis.

There are many strains of *T. gallinae*, not all of which are deadly. The most virulent form causes a buildup of crusty, whitish, necrotic lesions in the esophagus and mouth, which can prevent the bird from feeding or drinking, eventually causing death. It is spread among a susceptible population when infected birds pick up seed from feeders, or water from birdbaths, can't swallow it, and spit it out, so it is picked up by healthy birds.

Another disease found in many families of wild birds is avian pox, generally evidenced by sores or growths near the birds' eyes or on their feet. Caused by several strains of pox virus, it frequently leads to secondary infections and death.

A disease that hasn't yet reached Arizona, but which might within a few years, is mycoplasmal conjunctivitis, also called house finch disease, although it has also been seen in goldfinches. It was first noticed in the northeastern states, but has been spreading westward since.

All of these diseases are spread readily where birds congregate to feed or water—such as in your backyard. Occasionally, the Arizona Game and Fish Department will issue an alert on trichomoniasis to local newspapers when the disease reaches serious levels, usually during summer. During such times, homeowners are asked not to put out birdseed, and you should not even think about doing so. Those who ignore such a request for their own selfish interests put many, many birds at severe risk of sickness and slow death.

At other times, there are several prophylactic measures you can take to reduce the possibility of transmission. The protozoan that causes trichomoniasis is susceptible to desiccation, yet it also dies within a few hours if immersed in water. But it can live for several days on moist grain. A standard birdbath offers plenty of opportunity for transmission before the organism dies; so do standard birdseed feeders, with a trough of seed where many birds eat at once or right after each other. Consider alternatives such as running water and spreading seed widely on the ground.

All hardware stores sell quarter-inch copper tubing, which is used for supply lines to evaporative coolers. You can also buy a kit that includes the tubing and a saddle valve with a self-drilling point that attaches to almost any water pipe. The pipe leading to a hose faucet is a good source. With this kit you can run the tubing into your bird area and position it above some very small receptacle, like a rock with a depression in it. Adjust the valve so only a frequent drip comes out, and you've got a source of water the birds will love. Many will take showers under the drip. More important, it provides a constantly replenished source of water that is less likely to transmit disease. If you turn off the flow each night during disease alerts, the receptacle will dry out completely, further reducing the chance of contagion. You can build a similar arrangement using a misting attachment. Put this waterer in a tree well and the little excess will help irrigate the tree. However, small-diameter water pipes like these are prone to freezing, so protect them or turn off the water when it's cold.

Urban Raptors

The word *raptor* refers, broadly, to a bird of prey, which includes anything from magnificent golden eagles to peregrine falcons to sparrow-sized elf owls. We have several raptors that have either embraced the urban lifestyle or at least pay us a visit now and then.

Hawks and Falcons

Cooper's hawks seem to get along fine in cities, where they take advantage of tall, nonnative trees to nest and hunt their main prey, smaller birds. One survey turned up over eighty Cooper's hawk nests within the city limits of Tucson. Cooper's hawks are fairly small for hawks, about sixteen inches long, including the tail (like most raptors, females are noticeably larger than males). They are members of the genus *Accipiter,* a group of hawks with short, rounded wings and long tails, designed for maneuverability flying through thick cover. As adults, Cooper's hawks have a buffy breast and grayish back, with a long, barred tail, and red or orange eyes. They would be easy to identify except for our other local *Accipiter,* the sharp-shinned hawk, which looks confusingly similar. Sharp-shinned hawks are

A young red-tailed hawk is ready to test its wings on a nest outside Tucson.

on average smaller than a Cooper's (only twelve inches or so), and look very small indeed, with rapid wing beats compared to a Cooper's. But the sizes of the two can overlap. Cooper's hawks seem to be much more common, however—I probably spot eight or nine of them for every sharp-shinned I see.

Red-tailed hawks, the most common hawk across the United States, frequently wander into town, or can be spotted soaring above. Besides the distinctive reddish, fan-shaped tail, red-tails have a dark-brown head and dark-bordered wings when seen from below, with distinctive dark patches on the leading edge of each wing. (There is an uncommon dark morph color phase, too.) Red-tailed hawks are in another genus, *Buteo,* adapted for long, soaring flights. Red-tails hunt small mammals up to jackrabbit size, either while soaring or by watching from a perch. They'll also take lizards and snakes, and some birds.

One of the most fascinating hawks in southern Arizona is the Harris's hawk. Harris's are easy to spot: They're very dark with beautiful rusty shoulders and a white patch under the tail; when flying, the tail shows white bands at the base and tip. The feet and beak are yellow. Harris's are distinctive because they are one of only two cooperatively breeding hawks in the world (the other is the Galapagos hawk). Frequently, one or sometimes two of the previous year's young will stay with the parents and help raise a new brood. Thus you'll often spot Harris's hawks in threes, sitting on adjacent telephone poles or trees. They hunt together, ganging up on small mammals and quail in a coordinated pursuit.

The theories behind why cooperative breeding evolved—that is, why a young bird would waste a year of potential breeding energy to assist raising siblings—involve a lot of selfish-gene-type suppositions, but one simple idea is that the young birds that stay around gain extra experience in hunting before starting their own families; also, the cooperative hunting strategy seems to increase success and, thus, the amount of food available for all.

Harris's hawks reach the United States only in the southern parts of the Southwest (their distribution is centered in the tropics), so we're especially lucky to have them here.

The two largest falcons in Arizona, the prairie falcon and peregrine falcon, occasionally grace us with their streamlined presence, although neither is really suited to hunting within the confines of a city. Much more common in desert grasslands and near agricultural fields are American kestrels, diminutive falcons the size of a robin, about nine inches long. Kestrels hunt insects and mice from fence posts, or fly along and suddenly hover in one spot for several seconds, then dive on the target. Kestrels are one of the few raptors that display sexual dimorphism, a pattern difference between the sexes. Males have steel-blue shoulder patches lacking on females.

Owls

Great horned owls, which live in every state except Hawaii, adapt readily to city life, and many nest deep within Tucson. They generally appropriate

Great horned owls often nest within the city limits. These two fledglings will be hunting on their own soon.

the abandoned nest of a hawk. These are big owls with signature "horned" feather tufts, not mistaken for anything else around here, and at night call with a classic, deep *hoot, hoot, hoot.* Don't confuse real ones with those plastic things everyone puts on their roofs in utterly futile attempts to deter pigeons and other unwanted birds.

Smaller owls—the western screech owl and the lilliputian elf owl—are less common within the city limits, or at least much harder to find than great horned owls. Both are cavity nesters, often using old woodpecker holes in saguaros.

One other owl deserves mention: the burrowing owl. This little long-legged owl nests in burrows that can be ten feet long, usually in open fields. But I once found a pair nesting in a drain hole beneath a sidewalk in downtown Tucson, near the railroad tracks. They would come out each night to catch insects around nearby streetlights. I've also seen them in vacant lots elsewhere within the city, and along the fence surrounding the Davis-Monthan Air Force Base storage field. Burrowing owls can imitate

Burrowing owls nest on the edges of urban habitat.

the sound of a rattlesnake's rattle with a clarity that makes me jump every time. It surely must be an effective defense against predators that would otherwise try to dig them out.

To learn more about raptors, and to experience a breathtakingly close encounter with them on the wing, visit the Arizona-Sonora Desert Museum and take in the free-flight program, where you'll be circled and strafed by trained hawks handled by the staff. It's awe inspiring, and is guaranteed to make a raptor fan of you.

Watching Mammals

Mammals, for all their obvious evolutionary success, have never really gotten over a massive inferiority complex.

Remember, they evolved as furtive little rat-sized things scurrying around between the feet of reptiles hundreds of times their size. One wrong step and *splat*. The solution came naturally, along with the fur that, in part, made them what they are: They became not only furtive, but nocturnal. Problem solved, survival ensured, and the next thing you know, here we humans are, running the place. Maybe our attraction to nightclubs reflects some atavistic urge to celebrate a successful evolutionary strategy. Or maybe not.

In any case, a lot of mammals never abandoned either the furtive or the nocturnal lifestyle, which is why bird-watching is so much easier than mammal watching. Take an early morning walk through the desert and you might see a few rabbits, perhaps a coyote or two, and if you're really lucky, a deer, while in the meantime, hundreds of primary-colored birds have been flying back and forth in front of your face screaming *"Look at me! Look at me!"*

But the compensating factor is that seeing mammals, especially large ones, is significantly more thrilling than seeing even a lot of birds. Unless, of course, you're a helpless twitcher. My wife once led a group of real fanatics up Brown Canyon, their expensive German binoculars and Questar spotting scopes probing every which way for the canyon's rare avian specialties. At one point, Roseann spotted a perfect, fresh set of mountain lion tracks and a scrape—a mound of leaves and dirt that a lion urinates on as a territory display. She excitedly called the group around to show them where, just hours before, the most magnificent predator in the state had walked where they were standing. There was a smattering of muted "hmms," and "uh-huhs," and then someone shouted *"Sulphur-bellied flycatcher!"* and *poof,* they were gone.

For the rest of us, opportunities to watch mammals begin well inside the city limits—*if* you like rabbits. And they're more interesting than you might think.

Rabbits and Hares

Southern Arizona's Lagomorphs—the name for the order that includes rabbits, hares, and pikas—include two species of rabbit, the desert cottontail *(Silvilagus audubonii)* and eastern cottontail *(Silvilagus floridanus),* and two species of jackrabbit (hares), the blacktailed jackrabbit *(Lepus californicus)* and the antelope jackrabbit *(Lepus alleni).*

Jackrabbits and rabbits differ in a couple of significant ways. Rabbits dig burrows (or, often, appropriate abandoned ones of other species), and produce their young in nest chambers. Jackrabbits do little digging and generally have their litters aboveground, in a simple depression sometimes lined with hair. This lifestyle difference correlates with a developmental one: Newborn rabbits are altricial—that is, blind, naked, and helpless at birth—while newborn jackrabbits are precocial (not preco*cious,* as many people mistakenly say)—their eyes are open at birth, they're fully furred, and they can move around very soon thereafter. Makes sense, doesn't it? Baby jackrabbits are more exposed to danger, so they need to be able to escape on their own as quickly as possible. This also explains why jackrabbits have longer, stronger rear legs—they rely strictly on speed to evade predators, whereas cottontails usually just dodge for the nearest hole.

Desert cottontails (our other cottontail species, the eastern, is difficult to distinguish and occurs more at higher elevations, so it won't be on the quiz) live far within city limits in neighborhoods with large lots, where there's enough cover and food. You'll see them in the early morning grazing on lawns or browsing other plants. Their nest holes are difficult to find; when young are present, the female usually plugs the entrance when she leaves to forage.

Farther out toward the edge of town, where large vacant lots still offer running room, blacktailed jackrabbits, with their gigantic ears and kangaroo-like hind legs, will often sprint away from you from under a bush. If you look closely you'll find their "form": a shallow depression scooped out of the earth where they rest. In summer, jackrabbits use those enormous ears as heat radiators: They orient themselves to the north and angle their ears up in a direction that researchers have proved is the coolest quadrant of the sky. A dense web of blood vessels in each ear can then help dump excess body heat.

Even farther out in the desert, in south-central Arizona, you can spot a similar jackrabbit called the antelope jackrabbit. They can be distinguished from blacktailed jackrabbits, not by the tail (both have dark tails), but by their very pale, almost white sides. Even better—black*tailed* jackrabbits have distinctly black tips on their *ears*. Both of these jackrabbits are huge—up to eight pounds for the blacktailed, a couple more for antelope (versus two to three pounds for cottontails).

Ground Squirrels

My favorite in-town small mammal is the round-tailed ground squirrel (*Spermophilus tereticaudus*), the little tan guys you see running for holes alongside incredibly busy streets (the Spanish name for them is *juancito*—little johnny). I never paid much attention to them until I rescued a tiny, blind

You might find Harris' antelope squirrels stuffing their cheeks at your bird feeders.

infant from a cat years ago, and raised him starting with eyedroppers full of formula. He grew into the most tame and totally bonded wild animal I've ever had, scurrying around the house behind me and calmly sitting on my shoulder while I read, and begging (really! on his *hind legs*) for milk whenever I opened the refrigerator. He was also a one-man ground squirrel—when I first left him with my mother while I went on a trip, he tried to take her finger off the first time she reached into the cage. He astonished all my visitors for two and a half years before dying in his sleep, probably of a heart attack—he was as fat and sleek as an otter.

In less pampered circumstances, round-tailed ground squirrels dig extensive burrows, reaching about three feet deep, where the temperature can be seventy degrees or more cooler than surface temperature in summer. But you'll see them out on all but the hottest days, feeding on seeds and fresh plant growth. In winter, they seem to go into semihibernation, although they can still pop up on warm days.

If you see "chipmunks" in your desert yard, little bushy-tailed rodents with a light stripe down each side, you're probably looking at Harris' antelope squirrels (*Ammospermophilus harrisii*), actually a species of ground squirrel. They are active throughout the year, and they love fruit and spilled bird seed, with which they stuff their cheeks to comical proportions. They often stand erect to get a better view of their surroundings, and flick their tails constantly when alerted to some potential danger.

Coyotes

About where you start seeing jackrabbits and ground squirrels is also about where you'll start seeing coyotes (*Canis latrans*) with regularity. While coyotes make foraging runs astoundingly far into the middle of town, they need a bit more open space to actually live and breed. I've known of family groups doing well in the back lots of large in-town cemeteries, and in old sanitary landfills surrounded by development but with connections to major drainages. And, of course, coyotes do just fine all around the edges of suburbia.

The coyote of our southwestern deserts is a surprisingly small animal, averaging just twenty to twenty-five pounds as an adult, barely half what a coyote from the northeast might weigh (one Brando-esque monster from Maine bent the scale at sixty-eight pounds). This variation in body size is common among mammal species whose ranges encompass both warm and

The author sits next to a coyote den after the young have moved on. Coyote dens are generally very well hidden.

cold climates. Southwestern mule and white-tailed deer, bighorn sheep, and bobcats are all smaller than their relatives farther north. The physiology behind this variation is simple: An animal with less body volume has proportionally more surface (skin) area for radiant cooling, needs less water, and thus generally performs better in a hot climate.

Coyotes breed in February and March and have an average gestation period of sixty-three days—exactly the same as your domestic dog. Coyote dens are remarkably difficult to find, the small entrance hole well concealed in the bank of a wash or in a hillside. In April or May, the female gives birth to an average of five puppies, only a couple of which might survive to adulthood. Only the female and puppies use the den, and then only until the pups are weaned. Otherwise, coyotes are creatures of the open, sleeping wherever the mood hits.

Coyotes often congregate in slightly extended family groups that function as small packs. One or two of the year's young might stay around through the next breeding season, acting as big brothers and sisters to the new litter. These groups enhance hunting success and make it easier to defend territories but also use more resources. Family groups tend to be smaller in harsher environments or during periods of low productivity. Often in the Southwest, you'll spot a lone coyote or a pair watching you from just over a rise, where they can satisfy their curiosity but make a quick getaway if you do something unexpected.

While coyotes live nearly continentwide, their nightly chorus is inextricably linked with the West's wide-open spaces. A wolf's howl might strike us as somber, haunting, or plaintive, but the yipping, yapping, and crooning of a group of coyotes could never be mistaken for anything less than pure joie de vivre. And indeed, while coyotes howl for good territorial and bonding reasons, there is little doubt that they sometimes let loose just for the heck of it. We who are lucky enough to live where that sound can be a part of our lives rarely fail to find some of its joy transferred to us.

Then again—every now and then it seems a coyote has something to *say*. Our dog Robbie had never been bothered by, nor particularly interested in, coyotes calling. But one night a single coyote stood within about fifty feet of our house and let loose with a very complicated series of low woofs, growls, and barks, which totally freaked out the dog—he jumped into bed between us and tried to climb under the covers, something he has done only during close encounters with fireworks. Coyotes aren't supposed to have language, but we had no doubt this one was saying something about tomorrow's dinner special being filleted border collie with a light prickly pear glaze.

Foxes

Several other small carnivores frequent the fringes between suburban houses and undisturbed desert. Although normally secretive, they are more common than many people think.

The gray fox *(Urocyon cinereoargenteus)* is a beautiful small fox, only about eight pounds, patterned with black, gray and rust. Like the coyote, it's a consummate omnivore, consuming plant and animal material as each is available. Unlike coyotes, gray foxes are also consummate climbers, and in fact have semiretractable claws. They scale trees to forage for fruit as well as for birds. They're also great rodent hunters and have been known to excavate a den in one side of a kangaroo rat mound while the rats still occupied the other side. Sort of like having an apartment over a pizza parlor.

You might spot gray foxes trotting down dirt roads at night, apparently little disturbed by your vehicle. At other times they'll appear as a ghostly presence at the limit of a porch light's glow, watching you intently before vanishing. I've heard gray foxes make a number of vocalizations, ranging from yips and barks to a surreal noise that sounds like a mountain lion hacking up a fur ball. No, I've never actually heard a mountain lion hacking up a fur ball, but trust me, that's what it sounds like!

In lower, mostly flat desert scrub, an even smaller fox is identifiable by its outlandishly large ears. Kit foxes *(Vulpes macrotis)* are tiny, weighing at most four pounds, and almost totally carnivorous. Their range closely overlaps that of kangaroo rats, their preferred meal. Kit foxes like soft soil where they can easily excavate their extensive burrows, which usually have several entrances.

Bobcats

A more enigmatic, edge-of-the-city animal is the bobcat *(Felis rufus)*. I say enigmatic because bobcats always seem either to be invisible, or else they make a grand entrance strolling nonchalantly across the patio or golf course, often with a couple of kittens in tow. Nobody ever seems to spot one inadvertently.

Bobcats are widespread in the United States, but ours are small and rangy, often giving an appearance of being mostly legs. A big desert bobcat might weigh eighteen or twenty pounds—the weight of a very large house cat, but significantly taller. Bobcats are purely carnivorous, eating anything from snakes and rodents to rabbits and jackrabbits, with the Lagomorphs comprising up to half the diet.

Bobcats often show up in yards on the outlying edges of urban areas.

Bobcats, like all cats except African lions, are solitary except when breeding or raising young. Females can give birth at any time of year, although there seems to be a peak in spring. There are usually two kittens, but up to four are possible.

Deer

Deer are the largest animals commonly found near developments, and we are blessed with two species, the habitats of which overlap somewhat.

The desert mule deer *(Odocoileus hemionus)* is the bigger of the two, males reaching perhaps 150 pounds. Mule deer, in southern Arizona, are denizens of desert scrub, generally below four thousand feet (in northern Arizona, they inhabit pine forest at high elevations). The other, the white-tailed deer, is a subspecies of the widespread North American white-tailed deer, *Odocoileus virginianus,* called the Coues white-tail *(Odocoileus virginianus couesi).* Talk to three different experts and you will get three different authoritative assurances on how to pronounce "Coues." It's either "cows," "coose," or "cooze." (It refers to Elliott Coues, an ornithologist and naturalist who visited Arizona in the 1870s during a stint as an army doctor.) So take your pick—someone is sure to correct you. Anyway, Coues white-tail are graceful little deer, rarely exceeding one hundred pounds in weight; the females are waiflike things of perhaps sixty or seventy pounds. They are also, unless thoroughly accustomed to humans, very wary and difficult to get close to. They prefer higher ground than local mule deer, from around 3,500 feet up to the pine belt, concentrated in the oaks. In high desert, just below the point where a few oak trees begin to appear on the north slopes of hills, you can often find both species.

Besides a direct size comparison, there are a couple of ways to differentiate mule and white-tailed deer. When males have antlers (fully formed from around August into April, when they are shed), look carefully at the arrange-

Shed antlers of a Coues white-tail (top) and a mule deer (bottom), showing their relative configuration and size.

Coues white-tailed deer, such as this doe, are normally shy but can become acclimated to humans.

ment of points. White-tailed deer have a single main beam that sweeps forward over the face; the secondary points all grow up from this. Mule deer antlers grow as a series of forks, so you can't really distinguish a main beam. When startled, mule deer often run in a peculiar fashion called "stotting" (or "pronking," in Europe): They bounce with all four feet together. Color can help, too: I find white-tailed deer to be generally grayish, mule deer generally brownish. And of course there's the tail. White-tailed deer flash a big white flag when alarmed; mule deer have a skinny tail tipped in black. But both have pale rumps, so look closely.

Both species browse shrubs for most of their food, although they also do some grazing. Both tend to be most active in the early morning or evening, although they can be nocturnal, especially during full moons. During the day, they lie up under trees on hillsides or in ravines where they can watch the surrounding area for predators. Often deer—especially mule deer—will wait until a hiker is within a few yards before bolting with a fibrillation-inducing clatter.

Deer breed in December and January, and does give birth in July and August, to one or two fawns.

It's not necessary to do anything to attract deer, other than living near good habitat. They'll often become accustomed enough to people to wander into yards to browse (even white-tails). You could, if you chose, actively feed them—there are even commercial deer food preparations available—but it's best to leave them be. If you concentrate them too much, you might disrupt their normal patterns of behavior.

Insectivorous Bats

You have no idea what amazing animals bats are.

Imagine, just for a minute, that you are a female Mexican freetail bat flying into a nursery cave in the state of Sonora, Mexico. It's a medium-sized colony, home to perhaps twenty thousand other female bats, each of which has left a single offspring clinging to the roof of the cave, in densities of up to four hundred per square foot. So here you come after a night of foraging for insects, amid a stream of twenty thousand companions, all aiming for an entrance maybe four feet wide. As soon as you fly inside it is pitch dark and you can see nothing at all, but you continue flying, using as your only source of navigation chirps of sound you emit at up to fifty times per second, which bounce off the walls of the cave and off the other twenty thousand bats and return to your brain, which translates the data into a detailed three-dimensional image with resolution down to the thickness of a human hair (the proper term for this is *echolocation* or *sonar*—*not* radar, which involves electromagnetic waves). Remember—each of those other twenty thousand bats is emitting her own constant stream of chirps as well. In addition, those twenty thousand baby bats are all emitting *their* own chirps, calling to their mothers. Amid this unimaginable flood of noise you fly unerringly to your own offspring and suckle it (remember, you *are* a mammal).

If that sounds at all impressive, consider Bracken Cave in Texas, where approximately twenty *million* bats roost. Those twenty million bats eat nearly half a million pounds of insects. Every night. One colony in Arizona, near Clifton/Morenci, is nearly as large.

Here's an even more amazing fact about bat echolocation: It's *loud*. Some species transmit chirps that hit 120 decibels when they're in the open and ranging something far away—about like holding a squealing smoke alarm a foot from your ear. Fortunately, the frequency is far above our hearing range, so it does not affect us. Why isn't the bat deafened? Because the stapedius muscle in its middle ear *disconnects* the bones there (remember the hammer, anvil, and stirrup?) at the instant each chirp is broadcast. Told you they're amazing.

A water source can attract mammalian visitors large …

The order Chiroptera (which means hand-wing, a precise summation of a bat's wing construction) is an incredibly successful group of animals. About one in four of every mammal species on earth is a bat. That's well over nine hundred species. Worldwide, bats are divided into two major groups—the Megachiroptera, which comprises the giant, fruit-eating "flying foxes" of the old-world tropics, some with wingspans over five feet, and the Microchiroptera, which is everything else. In Arizona, we have twenty-eight species, two of which are nectar, pollen, and fruit eaters, the others of which all hunt insects or other small invertebrates. One of our bats, the pallid bat, frequently hunts on the ground, pursuing crawling bugs and even scorpions by simply listening for them. But most bats hunt in midair, using echolocation to snag insects on the wing. A single bat can catch more than one thousand insects in an hour.

Besides the two nectar-feeding bat species, which show up on the edges of urban habitat, five other species are the ones most commonly seen inside city limits, according to bat researcher Ronnie Sidner: the cave myotis (*Myotis velifer*), western pipistrelle (*Pipistrellus hesperus*), Mexican freetail (*Tadarida brasiliensis*), pallid bat (*Antrozous pallidus*), and big brown bat (*Eptesicus fuscus*). In summer, you stand a good chance seeing them on the wing at dusk, as they begin hunting. One of my favorite evening activities is sitting out with a drink and watching bats swoop and dive in unimaginably

...and small.

tight maneuvers as the last sunset light fades away. If you have a pool you might see bats drinking from it, angling down in a shallow dive and scooping up water on the wing.

Commercially manufactured bat houses have become quite popular in recent years, an encouraging sign that people are getting over fear of bats. Unfortunately, with a very few exceptions, bat houses put up in Phoenix and Tucson just don't work—it's simply too hot there. Residents of higher-elevation towns such as Bisbee and Oracle have a much better chance of success.

For more detailed information about the fascinating world of bats, buy a copy of *America's Neighborhood Bats,* by Merlin D. Tuttle.

Arizona has 138 mammal species, not including the one reading this. That leaves a whole bunch I haven't covered, including some you might see in urban or suburban settings. I suggest owning a copy of the *Peterson Field Guide to the Mammals of North America* to help you identify sightings, as well as the Arizona-Sonora Desert Museum's *A Natural History of the Sonoran Desert*. If you're really hungry for in-depth knowledge, invest in Donald Hoffmeister's *Mammals of Arizona,* which will tell you more than you'd ever need to know.

4

Reptiles and Amphibians

Okay . . . I know we're reaching the bottom on most people's wildlife watching preference list. But it's about time we grew out of our instinctive heebee jeebees and started admiring reptiles and amphibians for the amazing creatures they are. For the urban wildlife watcher, they're also very accessible: If you have a yard with a rock pile or a tree in it, or even just a wood fence, chances are you've also got at least a lizard or two in there. Farther out toward the edge of town you'll begin to find the odd snake as well, and summer puddles filled with tadpoles. Why restrict your enjoyment of animals to birds and mammals, when there's another whole class out there?

Lizards

The most ubiquitous reptile in Arizona cities is the tree lizard (*Urosaurus ornatus*), found throughout our state and in parts of all the other southwestern states. It's a small lizard, no more than six inches overall, with a mottled, dark pattern on its back. Tree lizards love trees, but you'll see them on walls and fences and in rock and wood piles too. The males often show bright blue-green belly patches when they do territorial "push-ups" to establish dominance. If you approach one that's clinging to a tree limb, it will escape by climbing higher while trying to keep the limb between you and it, occasionally peeking around the edge to see if you're still there.

Another common urban lizard—and a lot scarier to nonreptile persons—

Tree lizards *(Urosaurus ornatus)* are very common urban residents in southern Arizona. Look for them on mesquite and acacia trees, as well as walls and fences.

is the desert spiny lizard *(Sceloporus magister)*, a stocky character often described as "at least a foot long" by those unaccustomed to them. In truth, they rarely exceed eight or nine inches, but they do display a remarkably belligerent attitude, even toward humanoid bipeds three hundred times their weight. It's all bluff, however, unless you grab one, at which point it will deliver a painful nip (one attached itself to the nose of our inquisitive cat years ago, eliciting odd honking sounds from the cat until he managed to fling it off). Spiny lizards acclimate quickly to human presence, and will forage unconcernedly nearby while you sit on the patio. I know someone who trained one to clamber up his leg and take mealworms from his hand.

Desert spiny lizards, one of several similar species, have obviously spiny skin, and a dark wedge pattern under their throat. At higher elevations, mostly oak woodland, you'll find Clark's spiny lizards, which are generally lighter and have black bars on their forelegs.

Everyone's favorite desert lizard, the horned lizard (which, like most natives, I *still* call a horny toad), sometimes lives astonishingly deep within cities, exploiting abandoned lots and alleys. Although there are fourteen species of horned lizard in all, the only one you're likely to see within Tucson and Phoenix is the regal horned lizard *(Phrynosoma solare)*, the biggest of the bunch, about palm-sized as an adult. Horned lizards eat many kinds of small invertebrates, but several species specialize in ants, which they devour by the dozen with apparent impunity from stings and the bitter formic acid that deters most potential predators. Despite their fearsome appearance, with a head ringed in spikes, horned lizards are utterly harm-

The regal horned lizard (*Phrynosoma solare*) is the most common horned lizard in southern Arizona.

less to humans. In fact, if you pick one up and stroke it between the eyes, or turn it on its back and stroke its belly, it will frequently enter a trancelike state and not move for several minutes after you stop. If seriously harassed, however, a few species, including the regal, employ the startling defense of squirting blood in a thin but powerful stream from the corners of their eyes. While this might seem like a dumb thing to do to a possible predator, researchers have discovered that horned lizard blood contains a chemical that makes it distasteful to many animals, including dogs. The blood-squirting defense is so evolutionarily attuned to particular predators that it's difficult for a human to get the lizard to employ it.

The horned lizard's most obvious defense, that spiked head, is an effective deterrent against animals such as snakes that swallow their prey whole, but less so against others, such as raptors, that disassemble their meals first.

Many residents of Phoenix and Tucson find small, almost translucent lizards clinging to walls and window screens near lights on summer nights, hunting for insects, which they snatch with lightning-fast lunges. If you get close enough, you'll see that they also have vertical pupils, like a cat, bumpy

Western banded
geckos *(coleonyx
variegatus)* are active
on summer nights.

skin, and broad toe pads for climbing smooth surfaces. In midsummer, if you
look through a window screen at their underside, you can sometimes see a
pair of eggs inside the females right through their skin. These are Mediterranean geckos *(Hemidactylus turcicus),* which are native to Europe but have
been inadvertently introduced to many other places worldwide. They are
generally confined to urban areas here.

  Arizona also has a native gecko, the banded gecko *(Coleonyx variegatus),*
which is superficially similar but has smooth skin with transverse bands and
feet not adapted for climbing. Banded geckos seem altogether too fragile to
survive in the desert; they do so by being nocturnal and subterranean. If you
catch a banded (or Mediterranean) gecko, it will sometimes croak with
displeasure—one of the few vocalizations of any lizard.

  So—if you see a gecko on your wall, it's Mediterranean; if you find one
on the ground (typically under wood piles or rocks), it could be either. Look
for the bands and smooth skin to identify the native.

  One of my all-time favorite lizards, and one of the most fascinating reptiles on earth, is the whiptail *(Cnemidophorus* sp.), of which several species
can be found in Arizona. Whiptails are long and streamlined with light-
colored stripes and spots, and they move in quick, jerky sprints. They hunt
invertebrates on open ground and amid detritus from plants. What's fascinating is that eight of the thirteen *Cnemidophorus* species in the Southwest
are all-female. That's right, there are no males at all. The females reproduce
through a process known as parthenogenesis, essentially cloning themselves.

Whiptail lizards (*Cnemidophorus* spp.) of several species are all-female. They produce offspring by essentially cloning themselves.

We're not sure why parthenogenesis occurs so frequently in whiptails (it is known rarely among other reptiles, birds, and fish). As an evolutionary tactic, it's thought to give an advantage to a species colonizing a rapidly expanding habitat. Think about it: If you don't have to go through all the mating rigmarole, but can just go straight to the offspring part, you're way ahead of the game. Your population can theoretically grow at twice the normal rate, since every individual, not just half of them, can produce eggs. The chief disadvantage, and it's a biggie, is that if your environment changes, your species has no genetic variability to adapt to the changes, and might rapidly become extinct. Also, there is strong evidence that genetic variability is vital for staying ahead in the battle virtually every living organism wages against internal parasites. But for now, whiptails seem to be doing just fine.

Snakes

Snakes. The animal least likely to figure into most people's concept of "watchable" wildlife. And that's too bad, because snakes are cool. About

99 percent of all the herpetophobes I've ever met were able to get over it, at least to the point of being able to appreciate snakes on some philosophical level. That's a good start.

There are so many snake species in Arizona (around fifty) that I couldn't possibly offer an effective primer on identification here. Buy the Western National Parks Association's *50 Common Reptiles and Amphibians of the Southwest* and you'll be able to name most of what you'll see. Common snakes in southern Arizona suburbs include the gopher snake *(Pituophis melanoleucus)*, coachwhip *(Masticophis flagellum)*, common kingsnake *(Lampropeltis getula)*, long-nosed snake *(Rhinocheilus lecontei)*, patch-nosed snake *(Salvadora hexalepsis)*, and a couple species of rattlesnakes. Near open sources of water you can find garter snakes *(Thamnophis* spp.), and at night you might add night snakes *(Hypsiglena torquata)* and lyre snakes *(Trimorphodon biscutatus)* to the others you can encounter.

No matter which direction your personal prejudices may slither, remember that *all* snakes are vastly beneficial as controllers of their prey species, including rodents and invertebrates. As far as I'm concerned, the more snakes around, the better, and I'm always thrilled to see one slowly cruising the yard. Unfortunately, no one has yet invented a snake feeder. Imagine a big tube you could fill with kangaroo rats. . . .

Turtles and Tortoises

Turtles and tortoises are a much, much easier prospect for easy identification around here. Although Arizona has several native aquatic turtles, the only shelled reptiles you'll see crawling around are the western box turtle *(Terrapene ornata)* and the desert tortoise *(Gopherus agassizii)*. The desert tortoise gets much bigger than the box turtle, up to fifteen inches long versus six or so. But a small desert tortoise can look a lot like a big box turtle. The most obvious difference is in the shell. The box turtle's shell is hinged in front, so it can close completely over its head. The tortoise's shell isn't hinged; it draws its head in and folds its armored front legs over its face for protection. And the box turtle is found only in the southeastern part of the state, mostly in grasslands; its range just misses Tucson and doesn't reach Phoenix.

Desert tortoises are herbivorous, feeding on prickly pear fruit, grass, and other small plants such as mallows. Box turtles eat both plants and insects.

The desert tortoise *(Gopherus agassizii)* is the only tortoise you're likely to find near Tucson or Phoenix.

If you live near undisturbed habitat, it's quite possible you'll someday find one of these two crawling slowly along minding its own business. The best thing to do is leave it alone and enjoy the sighting. If you absolutely need to pick it up, say to move it out of a roadway, just keep your fingers away from its mouth, which can deliver a painful bite. Oh, and, especially in the case of desert tortoises, keep the rear end pointed away from you, as they'll sometimes void a putrid stream of waste when handled. But that "waste" is the contents of a reservoir of liquid that helps the tortoise avoid dehydration, so it's much better inside them than down your leg.

Toads

Lizards and snakes—even tortoises—figure so prominently in desert natural history lore that it's easy to forget their relatives, the amphibians. But we actually have plenty—they're just not out where you can see them all the time. Being generally genuinely slimy, amphibians might be even lower on the charisma scale than snakes. It's sort of the "Eeeewww!" factor versus the

Binoculars

I'll make a blanket statement here: Nothing will further your enthusiasm and enjoyment, and quicken your learning curve as a backyard naturalist (besides field guides), more than a good pair of binoculars.

But note I said "good," because few things are more frustrating than cheap, poor-quality binoculars. One morning a few years ago I was leading a natural history hike in the Baboquivari Mountains. With the group was a gentleman who had just bought a pair of fifty-dollar zoom binoculars from one of those discount chains with stores the size of junior college campuses. Being a gregarious sort, he immediately started teasing me about the fact that my Leicas were worth twenty times what his were, yet didn't even have a zoom (variable magnification) feature. I'd heard this all before, so I just smiled indulgently and waited. Presently I spotted something through my binoculars and said to the group, "Look at the beautiful Harris's hawk on that saguaro." I watched the gentleman peer through his binoculars at the hawk, which was perhaps 250 yards distant. He said, "How do you know it's a Harris's hawk?" I said, "Look at the rusty shoulders and the white band on the tail." He squinted again, fiddling with the focus and zoom knobs. Finally he frowned at me skeptically. I handed over the Leicas, which he took with an exaggerated, pinkies-out display of caution. He looked through them at the hawk, then looked at me, then back through the binoculars. Slowly he turned in a circle and scanned the canyon and horizon around us. At last he sighed, deeply and regretfully, and said, "Okay. I could get used to these."

Now, you don't have to spend a thousand dollars to get good binoculars. But the more you spend, the happier you'll be. I have never yet met a single person who regretted later having spent more on better binoculars. And the more you spend the more durable they will be, making higher quality also the thrifty choice in the long run. How's that for justification?

All binoculars are referred to with two numbers, such as 7 x 35 or 10 x 50. The first number refers to the magnification—how many times bigger they make an object appear. You'd think more would be better, but higher powers also magnify any shake in your hands, which can blur the image. Seven or eight power is ideal for most uses (avoid those zooms, which compromise optical quality). The second number refers to the diameter of the front, or objective, lens, in millimeters. Pocket-sized binoculars usually have 20 mm objective lenses or something close; midsize binoculars are around 30 mm, and full-size models are 40, 42, or even 50 or more. Bigger objective lenses gather more light, so they are brighter and render more contrast near dusk or in heavy shade, but they are also heavier, all else being equal.

If you just want a casual pair of binoculars, a pocket model is fine, but for all-around use, the midsize 30 mm (or thereabouts) objectives strike a good balance between brightness and light weight. Really serious naturalists and birders will go for full-size models.

Binoculars come in two basic configurations, depending on the arrangement of the prisms inside (prisms are located between the objective lens and the eyepiece, and fold the incoming light in a convoluted path, in part so your binoculars can be shorter than a telescope). Roof prism binoculars look like straight tubes, while porro prism models have a dogleg shape— the objective lenses are offset from the eyepieces. It makes little difference which you choose, although premium binoculars usually employ roof prisms for compactness and, probably, style.

The best way to buy binoculars is to try several pairs, at a store where the salespeople *know* about binoculars and can offer you real advice. Look through each model for as long a period as you can. If you have to readjust your vision when you take your eyes away, or if they feel strained, the optics are probably not very good. The view should be just like looking with your own eyes, except that everything is closer. If you need to wear eyeglasses while looking through the binoculars (if you have astigmatism, for example), ask for a model with long eye relief. If you're on a budget, $150 to $200 will buy you a decent instrument from Canon, Bushnell, Pentax, or Nikon. If you can afford the absolute best, look at Swarovski or Leica models. You won't be sorry. But be prepared to hear a lot of "Could I just use yours for a minute?"

"Aaaieee!" factor. But for a true desert rat (which can be made as well as born), the summer chorus of desert toads after a heavy monsoon rain is a life-affirming symphony, and a reminder of the ingenious ways in which animals have learned to cope with a harsh environment.

Our desert toads—the spadefoots (*Scaphiopus* spp.), red-spotted toads (*Bufo punctatus*), and the huge Sonoran Desert toads (*Bufo alvarius*) among them—can spend over 95 percent of their lives entombed beneath the ground with the outer layer of their skin desiccated to help seal in moisture (otherwise a toad can lose water forty times faster than a rattlesnake—not a good thing in the desert), with only tiny holes at the nostrils to allow oxygen intake. When summer rains form ephemeral pools, they dig their way out and begin advertising their presence and readiness to make new toads in no modest way. I've stood near pools that reverberated so deafeningly with croaks and trills that I had to shout to hear myself think.

The speed of the life cycle that follows the toads' emergence almost defies belief. Eggs of some species have been known to hatch in under fifteen hours, and the tadpoles that result morph into their adult toad shape within a week, ready to engage in a quick spurt of feeding before burying themselves. Two weeks after the rain and its puddles, nothing might remain to hint there was ever anything but dry dirt in the spot.

The closer to undisturbed desert you are, the better the chances you'll have high toad activity following a heavy summer rain. But you never know where the little buggers will show up—we stepped out to the porch of our university-area house one evening to find an enormous Sonoran Desert toad sitting contemplatively on the sidewalk. He eventually hopped ponderously down the side yard toward the wash, never to be seen again. And a friend told me of an active spadefoot population in a wash near Swan and Fifth Street in the middle of Tucson.

One caution about toads: They are extremely toxic to pets. In fact, a common defensive tactic of Sonoran Desert toads is to try to head-butt the

These tiny tadpoles have already developed legs.

animal investigating them, to make contact with the toxin-bearing glands. Keep your pets away from toads, and if they do come in contact, flush their mouth out thoroughly with a hose and keep an eye on their reaction.

Whether you live in the middle of town with a postage-stamp–sized yard, or on a multiacre spread bordering public land, there *will* be wildlife for you to watch and enjoy in southern Arizona. I have always been as tickled by the goldfinches and horned lizards that showed up in our university-area yard as I was by the deer and mountain lions that shared space with us while we volunteered on a wildlife refuge. They are all part of the same, awesome web of life that always finds niches to fill, no matter how modest the circumstances. So no matter which you have near you to enjoy—goldfinches or mountain lions—count yourself graced by their presence.

Pets, Orphans, and Collections

Growing up on the far northeast side of Tucson, near Sabino Creek and the foothills of the Catalina Mountains, with as-yet unbladed desert all around, I don't believe there was ever a time when my bedroom lacked some wild thing in a cage, jar, or terrarium. There were tadpoles, lizards, snakes (even, later, rattlesnakes), pocket mice rescued from cats, baby birds picked up off the ground and raised to adulthood, scorpions, and tarantulas. I once spent a month nursing a rock squirrel back to health after finding it near death with its eyes swollen shut, infested with some sort of bloodsucking mites that I picked off one by one. The morning it nearly took my finger off when I reached in the cage was when I realized it was ready to leave. (Which suggests a motto for wildlife rehabilitators: "When you can snatch the finger from my hand, it will be time for you to go.") I also had a messy collection of old nests, skulls, rocks, and various junk.

Wild Animal Pets

These days, conventional wisdom condemns such things. Wild animals, we are told, should be left in the wild and not imprisoned. In fact, conventional wisdom now dictates that *everything* should be left where it is, whether animal, plant, or inanimate object. We are taught to look, but not touch, when we go into the wild, to tread lightly, to take nothing but pictures and leave nothing but footprints. No exceptions.

Allow me to voice a cautiously dissenting view—one that I found I share with many, many naturalists, biologists, and teachers.

First, we should condemn without reservation the idea of trying to make large wild animals into pets, and particularly the fad trade in exotic animals designed to look cute and one-up the neighbor's exotic pet. I read an article some time ago that claimed there are more tigers kept as "pets" by wealthy individuals in the United States than there are tigers left in the wild. That's repugnant. On a more local level, people used to think nothing of capturing and raising bobcats, coatis, even mountain lions, often with tragic results for the animal. These are large, complex beings with extremely sophisticated patterns of behavior and instinct, and forcing them into a totally alien existence rarely succeeds.

Likewise, wholesale denuding of landscapes of rocks, plants, and other souvenirs would spell disaster, especially in heavily traveled state parks and national monuments.

On the other hand, we who care about the fate of wildlife and wild places in our country desperately need to inspire our children with the same love and respect we grew up learning. Those snakes and lizards I kept, the baby rodents I raised, the old birds' nests and skulls and rocks I collected, were what fed my love of the outdoors, made it an inseparable part of me, and inspired a lifelong determination to do whatever I could to protect what is left of the unspoiled parts of my home.

My fear—no, my *conviction*—is that if we teach our children they don't belong in nature, that they can only do harm there, that they must look, but remain apart and uninvolved, then they will simply *go do something else*. And that will be the beginning of the end of the wild.

Instead, our interaction with nature should be inspired by curiosity, fueled by passion, and tempered with respect and empathy.

When I lead natural history hikes for children or adults, I try to make the experience as hands-on as possible. We catch lizards and snakes to observe them closely, peer into old birds' nests, examine skulls and bones, and look under rocks. We're careful to put everything back exactly as we found it, but I make sure that everyone has a chance to not just look, but touch and smell and taste what is happening around them.

I suggest that, within the boundaries of the law, common sense, and concern for the welfare of the wildlife and the landscape, you should do the same, and encourage your children as well. You haven't seen wonder in a child's face until you share the experience of watching a chrysalis split and reveal the unfolding butterfly hidden within, which then flutters away when you open the lid of the jar. Such an experience has nothing in common with watching the same event on *Animal Planet*.

Many animals are legal to capture and keep in Arizona (although, for many, you need to possess a valid hunting license, oddly enough). I've never talked to any scientist who saw the slightest harm in capturing a snake or lizard, keeping it for a couple of weeks, and then letting it go in the same spot it was captured. Children are fascinated watching the movements of such animals, which adapt within days to captivity. I've occasionally kept snakes permanently that seemed to do particularly well. One night snake I caught in a housing development tamed instantly, fed readily on fence lizards, and was a perfect, calm subject for introducing children's groups to snakes. It grew long and fat over eight or nine years, and I finally passed it on to my niece, who still has it.

Smaller animals and even some insects can be kept easily if you know their food preferences. It's simple to find caterpillars feeding on their host plants and install them in a big jar, with a replenished supply of the plant to feed on. Then the trick is to catch them in the act of spinning a cocoon, or emerging as a moth or butterfly.

Orphaned or Injured Wild Animals

Orphaned animals present a different situation to one where we keep a snake for a few days, or watch the transition of a caterpillar. The first necessity is determining if the animal is really orphaned. Countless "orphaned" animals are brought to zoos and wildlife rehabilitation centers each year by well-meaning but ignorant people who don't recognize a fawn that is curled up simply waiting for its mother to return from foraging, or a bird that has fallen from the nest but is being fed by its parents. Unless the animal has been brought in by someone's cat (the source of probably three-quarters of all my patients through the years), it's almost always better to wait and watch to see if a parent returns.

If you see a baby bird on the ground that's still unable to hop much, look above it to see if you can see the nest it might have come from. There's no harm in picking up the hatchling and placing it back in the nest—most birds have very little sense of smell and won't reject such a returned offspring. If the bird is partially fledged and able to run or fly for a short distance, you're better off leaving it alone than terrifying it by chasing after it.

Young small mammals, such as round-tailed ground squirrels and mice, sometimes crawl out of their nests before they should. I've actually tracked the little things backward and located where they belonged, and stuffed them back inside. But an obviously abandoned individual presents a quandary. Taking it in and attempting to raise it yourself is an extremely time-intensive process, and the mortality rate for such attempts is always very high—just as is the natural mortality for such animals. But there are books on the subject that tell you how to proceed, and provide recipes for correct food mixtures (warm skim milk won't do it). The best one I ever found is *Care of the Wild Feathered and Furred,* by Mae Hickman and Maxine Guy, which is still in print. Mice and round-tailed ground squirrels both seem to adapt readily to a captive existence, and any commercial rodent house will suffice as a home.

Larger animals are much more problematic, and not candidates for home rearing. You should be absolutely certain they are orphaned or injured before interfering at all—and many scientists would say not even then. Your best bet is to call a wildlife rehabilitator for advice.

Many injured-animal stories have a happy ending. Shortly after we were married, my wife and I found a western screech owl by the side of a road, obviously stunned from a collision with a car. One of the bird's eyes had a nasty looking contusion. I caught it and we took it to the Arizona-Sonora Desert Museum, which accepted it but warned that they could not keep us informed of its fate. Eventually we stopped wondering, until at least five years later, when on a visit to the museum we spotted a docent with a very composed little screech owl perched on her glove—a screech owl with a peculiar dark spot in one eye. That owl had not only survived, but had helped educate hundreds of people, and seeing it brightened our whole month.

Collecting Wild Keepsakes

Of course, it's not only live animals that can inspire us and maintain a sense of connection to the wild. My office is the logical descendant of my childhood bedroom and, I like to think, an extremely modest descendant of the study of one of the nineteenth-century British explorer-naturalists, those men of independent wealth and indefatigable energy who reached the ends of the earth and brought home a good portion of it. There are old nests, skulls and skeletons, skins, rocks, saguaro boots, generally a snake or two temporarily on loan from the wild, antlers, a root that looks startlingly like a snake, and hundreds of other bits. Every piece brings back the memory of where it came from and what I was doing at the time. Each bone or nest is a microcosmic slice of the animal that grew it or built it, and serves as a mnemonic trigger that recalls a flood of information about that species. The whole room is a visual and tactile connection to nature.

Even with inanimate objects, though, one must be careful not to flaunt any laws. Those protecting raptors and migratory birds are particularly unbending, and a single hawk feather picked off the ground could result in big trouble. Worse trouble yet is possible: Once, while sea kayaking in the Sea of Cortez, I picked up a perfectly preserved and sun-bleached skull of a male sea lion, with a magnificent sagital crest and a full set of imposing teeth. It sat out on my shelf for years with two dozen other skulls until, stupidly, I left it out on a shelf in a house we were caretaking that belonged to the U. S. Fish and Wildlife Service. A visiting supervisor from Washington noticed it and, graciously, suggested I get rid of it. Since he could easily have had me tossed in the slammer for violating the Marine Mammal Protection Act, I sheepishly and readily complied.

Such laws might seem capricious, but they are sorely needed to prevent wholesale slaughter of threatened species. Still, I'd like to see a modicum of flexibility built into some of them. A few years ago in Arizona, the newspapers reported the story of a young man who had raised an orphaned raven, which grew into an intelligent and totally bonded pet. Unfortunately, the Arizona Game and Fish Department found out about it. Since captive ravens are illegal, the department confiscated the bird . . . and destroyed it. That didn't make much sense to me, and I'm certain even less to the young man. Perhaps we'll learn from such incidents and return to a philosophy that encourages our young people to get involved with nature.

If you'd like to be inspired as a naturalist, find a copy of Gerald Durrell's wonderful *The Amateur Naturalist*. It's full of projects suitable for adults or children. Remember: The important thing is to *get involved* with nature.

Part 2

Avoiding Wildlife Problems

Introduction
There Are No Problem Animals

First, let's agree on a ground rule: There is no such thing as a "problem animal." It is we humans who are the problem—after all, the animals were here first, and it is we who move into their territory and then demand elevated standards of behavior from them, or even insist that they leave altogether. And the "problems" animals cause us are invariably simply side effects of their going about their lives: looking for food, building nests or dens, or marking or defending their territory. Furthermore, many "problem" animals are actually beneficial to us until a single incident disrupts things. A rattlesnake might spend years invisibly controlling the population of woodrats around a home until it curls up on the porch one morning and scares the owner out of his pajamas.

But we have to be realistic. Humans are here to stay. And even the most committed and placid of animal lovers have become first frustrated, then maddened, and, yes, finally driven to murderous rage after having gardens repeatedly torn up, car wiring chewed through, or stored linens shredded. I have a friend who is the classic Birkenstocked liberal vegetarian greenie, who had a pair of Gila woodpeckers decide that her new wood-sided addition was the perfect place for a condo. After the fifth or sixth ragged hole appeared in the building, I believe she would have gleefully twisted the heads off both those birds if she could have caught them. And how many pacifist million-mom-marchers have entertained fantasies of buying a shotgun when woken for the twentieth time at 5:00 A.M. by one of those same woodpeckers advertising its territory with an exuberant BRADADADADADADAT on a metal roof vent?

Nevertheless, although this chapter will suggest various methods of dealing with what I'll go ahead and treat as nuisance animals, the guiding philosophy I will stress is tolerance. Remember, in your dealings with the wildlife around your home, that every single animal there has a function and has evolved in an interdependent relationship with other species. If you find the behavior of some animal annoying, stop and think for a moment. Is it really doing something annoying, or if *you* weren't there to be annoyed would it be just another creature minding its own business? Would something as simple as a change of attitude on your part make the problem go away? If so, the honorable thing to do is to give the animal a break.

If, on the other hand, an animal is causing property damage, or is a threat, real or perceived, to your safety or that of your family or pets, you'll probably be inclined to take more drastic action. The traditional approach to such problems has been to simply kill the offending animal, and, indeed, in certain rare circumstances, such a solution might be the only reasonable choice. But keep one very important rule in mind: When you kill a mouse, woodrat, bird, or snake—or even a javelina or a mountain lion—and do nothing else to mitigate the circumstances that attracted that animal in the first place, another one is *certain* to take its place, and you will be caught up in a perpetual cycle. It's much more effective—and a lot easier on the wildlife—to take a preemptive role and prevent problems, instead of simply reacting to them. This axiom holds true whether you're a homeowner battling woodpeckers or a rancher losing calves to predators.

We can divide problem-causing animals into three very general groups. First, and of most concern, are those that can physically harm us, such as rattlesnakes, scorpions, black widow spiders, and the like, as well as those that can harm our pets—coyotes, owls, javelina, and such. Second are those that cause property damage: mice, woodrats, woodpeckers, and so forth. Last are the mere nuisances—which, ironically, often raise tempers the highest. I got extremely annoyed at one of my best friends, a late sleeper, who bitterly complained at the "racket" made by a mockingbird singing outside his bedroom window at 7:00 in the morning. My sympathy was, to say the least, limited. (Then again: In Brown Canyon, we were able to confirm the summertime presence of buff-collared nightjars, a species extremely high on the want list for American birders, and very rare north of the Mexican border. Buff-collared nightjars have an unmistakable call that sounds a bit like someone pouring wine from a bottle, and we were delighted when one woke us up at 2:00 one morning, singing about five feet from the bedroom window. By the fifth straight night, however, we had passed delight, and were considering emotions less joyful, when the bird finally moved on.)

However, just dividing animals into "hazardous," "destructive," and "aggravating," or something like that, would do exactly what I'm hoping to avoid: force them arbitrarily into categories of our own prejudicial making. So we'll just leave them where they belong, in their natural groups: reptiles, mammals, and so on. Remember, *there are no problem animals!*

Birds

Well, just one bird, really: everyone's favorite alarm clock and building ventilator, the Gila woodpecker. (Street pigeons are beyond the scope of this book. If I *were* to offer advice on those, it would be along the lines of a 20-gauge pump.)

Out in the desert where we aren't there to be annoyed at them, Gila woodpeckers are true Arizona birds, almost entirely restricted in their U.S. range to the southern part of our state, where their favorite residential plant, the saguaro, grows. Gila woodpeckers bore nest holes into the outer, fleshy part of the saguaro, forming a cavity shaped like a vase with the opening bent over to the side. The saguaro exudes a callus material that hardens and seals in the nest, leaving a cozy, well-insulated retreat used by many other birds after the woodpecker abandons it, including elf and screech owls, kestrels, and even purple martins.

Interestingly, the Gila woodpecker usually bores its nest in the fat, lower parts of the saguaro's limbs, and does not go through the woody skeleton. As a result, the cactus normally suffers little permanent damage. But another local cavity nester, the gilded flicker, bores its holes much higher on the limbs, and often chisels right through the skeleton, sometimes seriously weakening the structure.

The hard nest lining produced by the saguaro often outlasts the cactus itself, leaving the "saguaro boots" so popular with desert rats. Human ones, that is. The *really* interesting part is that it takes several months for the saguaro to form the casing around the freshly excavated nest, before which it cannot be used. So the woodpeckers you see boring nest holes in saguaros are building *next year's* nests.

A saguaro boot.

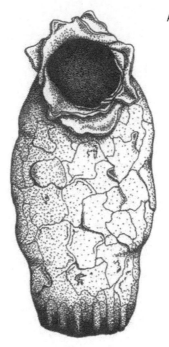

Gila woodpeckers also use cottonwoods, willows, and large mesquite trees for nest holes. In cities, they'll happily substitute buildings.

I think of Gila woodpeckers as a sort of avian architecture critic for the Southwest. See, the classic colonial or pueblo styled building, built from red brick or adobe, with a parapet wall extending above a flat, sloped roof, is nearly immune to attack from Gila woodpeckers. When we introduced styles from other areas of the country, and started building with cheaper materials like plywood—*that's* when the trouble began. A peaked roof with a wood gable under each end, common on bungalows and the newer California-style row houses, looks to a woodpecker like a gigantic covered porch with a blank canvas of hole-boring matrix. Wafer-board storerooms and additions are nearly as attractive. I once sat and watched a bird pound a perfectly round hole in a neighbor's frame-and-plywood guest house in less than a half hour.

It *is* possible to stop woodpeckers from attacking these materials. First, if they can't get a foothold, they can't drill. A clear wall section of that fake tongue-and-groove plywood, if it's sanded smooth and painted with semigloss paint, won't allow the birds to land. But if there's trim around the perimeter they can grip, or if you put a nice window frame right in the middle, they'll hang off it like a Yosemite free-climber and go to work.

On new construction, there are a couple of ways to prevent damage. The simplest is to stucco over expanded metal lathe instead of using plywood. But one remodeler I worked with rebuilt a garage gable end for a client who liked the tongue-and-groove look. We stapled expanded metal *underneath* the plywood to see what would happen. The paint had hardly dried before a woodpecker went to work. However, when it got a small hole drilled through the wood and ran into the metal, it gave up and tried another spot. Same result. After one more attempt, the bird moved on, and the plywood required only minimal patching. It was still a yearly task to mend the trial holes, but the birds were unable to complete a full-sized nest opening.

If you have an existing building with an area where Gila woodpeckers drill, screwing strips of galvanized sheet metal over the spot will stop them. Done neatly and painted to match, you can hardly tell it's there from a distance. Be careful when you install the metal, however, that you don't give the birds a new foothold at the edge of it, or they'll just move the drilling operation outward. If the rest of the building is stuccoed, you can also install metal lathe and extend the stucco to cover the wood.

Note that dissuading woodpeckers by scaring them off rarely works for long. Fake owls are effective for about a day, after which the birds treat them as a nice perch. If you move the owl every few days, it might remain effective, but who wants to do that? Similarly, bright flashing metal strips or ribbons become part of the scenery to birds very quickly, and hardly add to the aesthetics of your home.

When woodpeckers bore holes in wood siding, it might be destructive, but at least it's relatively quiet, unlike their other habit. Gila woodpeckers advertise their territory by rapidly hammering on anything that amplifies the sound. And few things do so better than a metal vent pipe with a fifteen-hundred-square-foot resonating chamber (your house) attached to it.

Fortunately, this activity is largely a springtime phenomenon. It's also easy to foil, as I've done for several acquaintances (my wife and I rise as early as the woodpeckers, so their hammering only amuses us). I make a cylinder out of half-inch hardware cloth, with a top cut from a circle of the same material and crimped to the cylinder. This device needs to be big enough in diameter, and tall enough, to enclose the vent pipe in question and stand off from it about three inches, especially at the top where the rain guard is. I

A Gila woodpecker
prepares to wake up
the neighborhood.

attach the cylinder to the vent with stiff wire so it can't blow off or blow up
against the side of the vent. With this in place, the function of the vent isn't
hindered, but the birds are. They can't reach the metal pipe with their beaks
to hammer on it, and will find another vent—with any luck, one on your
neighbor's house. Incidentally, hardware cloth caps are also effective at
preventing birds from falling down chimneys.

Occasionally, Gila woodpeckers will hammer on metal evaporative coolers or roof-mounted air conditioning units. This is more difficult to stop,
although it's also generally not nearly as loud as the vent pipe hammering.
Evaporative coolers can be enclosed with a canvas cover, which, since most
of the hammering happens in spring, can then be removed to use the cooler
when the weather warms up in May. Air conditioning units are more
difficult, especially since so many of them incorporate heat pumps for winter use and thus must be left uncovered. But if you have a real problem, it's
not very difficult to make a larger, square version of the vent cover, with a
wood frame, that can be dropped over the whole unit. Make it in flat sec-
tions that can be wired together into a cube, then stored flat.

A Gila woodpecker snags some hummingbird food before doing some territorial drumming.

With your house thus armored, you shouldn't have many problems with Gila woodpeckers. Of course, they'll still perch outside your window at 6:00 A.M. and let loose with that EEK!EEK!EEK!EEK! call. That, I suggest you learn to enjoy.

Reptiles

Snakes

A debate has simmered for decades about whether the fear of snakes is instinctive or learned. For every video I've seen showing infant monkeys reflexively cowering at the sight of a cobra, there's another that shows a human baby cooing and giggling while *petting* a cobra. Just kidding. I meant "while petting a harmless king snake." But I'll bet it made you jump. Was that instinctive or learned?

In any case, the fear of snakes—or reptiles and crawly things in general—once acquired, is difficult to shed. My mother never entirely got over hers, in spite of near-constant exposure to the legless residents of my bedroom. But at the other end of the spectrum is a dear friend from Virginia who, determined to conquer her herpetological heebee jeebees after moving to Arizona to teach, signed up to work on a reptile survey—sort of the total immersion treatment. Boy, did it work, too: Not only is she now completely comfortable around reptiles, she refers to individuals with adjectives such as "precious," and cuddles them and names them. Kind of weird, actually.

I could offer all the standard intellectual reasons why fear of snakes is unreasonable: They aren't cold and slimy, but dry and pleasantly cool to the touch; they perform a valuable service as rodent controllers, and so on. But the operative word in the phrase above is *unreasonable*—the fear of snakes often doesn't respond well to logical arguments. Many people have the sense to appreciate that snakes are beneficial, but still can't overcome their revulsion. If you're one of them, the best thing you can do is to spend some time experiencing snakes in a comforting environment, such as at the Arizona-Sonora Desert Museum, both in the reptile room and especially at docent demonstrations. Or sign up for one of those surveys.

One of the first questions people ask when they begin to learn about snakes is "*Why?*" That is, why would evolution design an animal with no legs and a long, slithery body? Since we're pretty certain that snakes evolved from ordinary, leg-equipped lizards sometime around 150 million years ago, there must be some benefits, and indeed there are. In essence, snakes can hunt in places where legs would be an impediment rather than an advantage. This includes underground (one snake-origin theory is that the first snakes were largely fossorial) and amongst thick brush and litter. It works so well that some lizards have adopted a legless existence too. And to answer your next question, "What the heck is the difference between a snake and a legless lizard?": There are several differences between snakes and lizards besides what you thought was the obvious one. Snakes have no movable eyelids and no external ears, and they possess a lower jaw structure modified to allow them to swallow large prey items whole. Snakes also shed their skins in one piece, while lizards do so gradually, in many pieces (somewhat like you).

In southern Arizona, snakes are most active from spring through fall. But it's possible to encounter them in any month of the year if the weather is warm enough. During the hot months they are mostly nocturnal, but you'll find them moving in the early morning.

All snakes are predators, and all are highly beneficial. An average gopher snake might eat a woodrat every week or two; a smaller king snake will account for an equal number of mice. Whether or not you like rodents, the simple fact is that, without control, their numbers would quickly explode to plague levels.

Nonvenomous Snakes

Arizona is blessed with over forty species of nonvenomous snakes, ranging from worm-sized blind snakes to gopher snakes seven feet long. Their diets span a similar range, from tiny invertebrates to rabbits. And they are found from the lowest deserts to the tops of ten-thousand-foot mountains. Many species inhabit developed areas and are occasionally spotted by residents crawling across roads or yards.

And what should you do if you find a nonvenomous snake in your yard, and you don't want it there? Nothing. Sorry, this one's non-negotiable. A snake is one of the best natural tools in existence for controlling things you *really* don't want around, such as mice and woodrats. Snakes are quiet, clean, and do no damage. Nonvenomous snakes can't harm pets or children (although, of course, children should be taught to stay away from *all* snakes until they are old enough to positively differentiate them). Snakes are completely nonaggressive: If you spot one and it spots you, too, its only instinct will be to escape. And it's quite likely that you'll never see it again, since snakes range around a territory much bigger than your yard.

If you move into an area where snakes are present, and insist on having them removed because of your own deep-seated prejudices or fears, you should know that translocated snakes are at much greater risk of dying from starvation or predation (see the section on rattlesnakes). This is, quite simply, indefensible and highly irresponsible.

Even if you *like* snakes, and are concerned about other people killing them or accidentally running over them, the odds are that they're better off left alone rather than moved to a strange territory, even one in an undeveloped area.

Venomous Snakes

Coral snakes. The Sonoran coral snake *(Micruroides euryxanthus)* is always referred to in awed tones by those who have learned just a little about snakes: "You know, they have the same venom as a *cobra*." Which is true enough to have earned the poor little coral snake an utterly undeserved reputation. But even though they belong to the same family as cobras, the Elapidae, which also boasts such fearsome members as mambas and kraits, there are a couple of significant differences between your archetypal elapid and our Sonoran coral snakes.

First, an average *M. euryxanthus* could coil up in your palm with room to spare, and a monster individual might reach twenty inches in length. This scale extends to the coral snake's head, which is very narrow, and its mouth, which is tiny. Inside that mouth are fixed fangs (not movable like a rattlesnake's) barely as long as the *i* in *miniscule*. So a coral snake has a difficult time inflicting a penetrating bite anywhere but on the finger of an adult human.

Sonoran coral snakes are also extremely retiring, mostly nocturnal, and spend a great deal of time underground. In decades of *looking* for snakes of all kinds, I have found perhaps two dozen coral snakes. When cornered, rather than striking they often coil up with their head buried and their tail waving in the air as a distraction, and sometimes do not attempt to bite even if handled. They also employ an additional defense, which generates disbelief among those first exposed to it: They fart. It's true—by everting the cloaca rapidly, a coral snake draws in and then expels forcefully a tiny bubble of air, emitting a sound like a miniature version of, well, you know. A series of these absurd little pops, emerging from a tail waggling at you like a rude clown face, is enough to reduce a circle of onlookers to helpless mirth, at which point the snake unwinds and dashes for a hole. Well, I don't suppose that's actually the strategy, but it works.

Because of their shy nature, surprisingly little is known about coral snake biology. They feed on small reptiles, especially the wormlike blind snakes of the genus *Leptotyphlops*. The coral snake's normal hunting mode is to simply seize the prey, inject venom, work its mouth around to the head of the victim, and start swallowing.

But with all this said, the tiny amount of venom produced by coral snakes does, indeed, contain a very potent neurotoxin. There are vanishingly few records of coral snake envenomization on humans, due to the reasons outlined above, but from those bites that have been documented (*all* of them apparently on people who were handling the snake at the time), the victims reported numbness and pain in the bitten finger and hand, nausea and drowsiness, and disorientation. That's enough to make it clear that coral snakes shouldn't be handled, and that children should be kept well away from them.

Fortunately, coral snakes have a lovely built-in warning mechanism in their brilliant bands of color: red, yellow, and black. While many harmless snakes share these colors, very few share the sequence, leading to the folk axiom, "Red on yellow kills a fellow; red on black venom lacks." That is, on coral snakes the red and yellow bands touch, but the red and black bands don't; on most harmless snakes, the red and black bands touch. Even among snakes that do show the same sequence, such as shovel-nosed snakes and long-nosed snakes, there are other ways of differentiating. Coral snakes have very even bands of color that wrap all the way around the body, while shovel-nosed snakes have red and black saddles on a yellow or creamy background. Craig Ivanyi, curator of herpetology at the Desert Museum, suggests that coral snake identification approaches 99 percent certainty by adding together these three characteristics: black on the nose extending behind the eye, red-on-yellow pattern, and bands that completely encircle the body. But, needless to say, it's much wiser to leave alone any snake with a red, yellow, and black pattern. And, of course, you can always listen for farting.

Rattlesnakes. Rattlesnakes are without doubt the most misunderstood, feared, and abused animals in the Southwest. They've been shot, beheaded, stomped, and run over on sight since Europeans first laid eyes on them. They've been cast as villains in hundreds of movies and books. And the shadow of our fear has a long reach: Countless nonvenomous snakes are killed each year by edgy homeowners and hikers who mistake them for rattlesnakes.

Yet when one attempts to track down some facts to bolster this fearsome reputation, the evidence proves thin indeed. Consider: Various sources report that about eight thousand people are bitten by venomous snakes each year in the United States (including nonrattlesnake species, such as copperheads and water moccasins). But of all those bitten, only five to eight die. That's a mortality rate of one in one thousand. But there's more. Well over half of the victims were *handling* the snake at the time, which is like playing with a loaded and cocked pistol and becoming a "gunshot victim" when you put a bullet through your foot. In fact, a significant spike in the demographic chart of snakebite victims occurs at the point where "Victim profile: young male" intersects "Contributing factor: alcohol." Uh huh. (As an aside, Craig Ivanyi told me that "tattoos" are also listed as statistically significant. Make of that what you will.)

Furthermore, statistics can be wrong. Try to find the source for the putative eight-thousand-venomous-bites-per-year and you'll get lost in an involute circle of references. It seems that everyone who quotes the figure is quoting someone else who quoted it from someone else. The real number is hard to pin down, because snake bites don't have to be reported to any federal agency, but it's almost certainly much lower. One documented report, for 1994, compiled by the National Association of Poison Control Centers, lists 1,328 bites and two deaths. Dr. David Hardy, one of the top authorities on rattlesnakes in the country, believes the average figure is indeed significantly lower than eight thousand, possibly averaging up to three thousand, but admits that "it's just a guess."

Certainly, five to eight—or even two—deaths per year is no laughing matter. But statistically it's a microbe, a quark, a neutrino on the list of dangers to concern yourself with. It's common, when one wants to downplay

Black-tailed rattlesnakes such as this one are generally found in higher-elevation habitat.

some risk, to quote *another* risk to put it in perspective. The popular one among herpetologists is that you're twenty times more likely to be killed by lightning than by a rattlesnake. But the lightning comparison is sort of passé stat-crunching. So I extrapolated another one: Discount the fatalities among the "reptile wranglers" who were, arguably, asking for it, and, as a U.S. citizen, you are as likely to be killed by a falling vending machine as by a rattlesnake. It's true; you can look it up. (Intriguingly, intoxicated young males figure just as predominantly in vending machine mishaps as in snake bites. Uh *huh*.) There's another important parallel here: Neither a vending machine nor a rattlesnake is likely to hurt you unless you mess with it.

Of course, statistics and vending machines are of little relevance when you step out your back door and find a nice fat diamondback crawling slowly across the porch, or curled up under the geraniums. What then?

Natural history. Rattlesnakes belong to a subfamily of snakes called Crotalinae, the pit vipers—so named because of the small cavity visible just behind each nostril (I don't suggest getting close enough to the one on the porch to check this out). These pits are infrared receptors, informing the snake of the proximity and direction of warm-blooded prey—it's been demonstrated that a rattlesnake can strike accurately at a mouse in complete darkness. The venom delivered in that strike is stored in glands behind each eye, and directed through hollow fangs attached to specialized maxillary bones in the upper jaw, which allow the fangs to pivot from flat against the jaw to a stabbing position when the mouth is opened. Incidentally, as a (possibly) interesting semantic point, the word *venom* is the proper one to describe what a rattlesnake injects. Technically, a *poison* is something that must be ingested. But even herpetologists slide on this one.

It's important to remember that the rattlesnake's venom evolved primarily as a tool with which to secure food, and is thus vastly more effective at offing mice or woodrats than people. Only secondarily does the venom deter predators. The snake's real defensive mechanism—besides excellent camouflage—is its rattle, which serves to warn animals near and large enough to be dangerous that "If you don't leave me alone, I'll bite you and you'll be sick and in a world of hurt for a long time." The warning served well for millennia (explaining why burrowing owls, which nest in burrows and are vulnerable to many of the same predators as rattlesnakes, imitate the sound with unnerving precision). However, with the arrival in the New World of Europeans, the combination of venom and rattle took on negative

You never know where a rattlesnake might decide to coil up.

survival characteristics. Venom = Bad; Rattle = Signal to grab a shovel or unholster the Colt. Fortunately, most of us are now aware that rattlesnakes have a proper place in the grand scheme, and gratuitous snake killing has fallen out of fashion. (Mostly. The infamous "rattlesnake roundups," where hundreds and hundreds are killed as spectacle, are still depressingly common in some states.)

There are, depending on which taxonomy you subscribe to, thirteen or fourteen species of rattlesnake in Arizona—more than in any other state. But the two most commonly encountered in southern Arizona by homeowners (and hikers, as well) are the western diamondback and the Mojave, with black-tailed rattlesnakes and a couple others somewhat behind.

Encountering a rattlesnake. So—you've just stepped out the door in your new suburban house and there's a nice fat rattlesnake crawling across the porch. What are your options? Essentially, there are three: You can leave it alone, you can move it, or you can kill it. The best solution will depend on several variables.

First, if you see a rattlesnake and just step back in the house for a few minutes, there's a very good chance that when you come back out the snake will be gone and you'll never see it again. Rattlesnakes don't normally spend a lot of time out in the open, and they're most likely to hunt where prey is to be found. Since the normal home range of a rattlesnake can range from an area a couple hundred yards on a side to over a mile, the space taken up by your house might be a minor portion, and not chanced upon again.

The leave-it-alone option is a good first strategy, especially if you are tolerant of snakes in general, and don't have small children or pets running around outside. However, what if it becomes obvious, through repeated sightings, that you have a permanent resident? Several factors might contribute to this possibility. First, your house could simply be in the middle of the snake's preferred habitat. Or, if you have mice, woodrats, or ground squirrels nesting close to the house, snakes will be able to detect them and will be more inclined to hang around looking for a meal. Also, many people don't realize that many rattlesnakes (particularly, according to David Hardy's studies, diamondbacks) happily eat birds as well, so the presence of a bird feeder can attract rattlers too. One tagged rattlesnake I know of, having discovered a smorgasbord beneath several bird feeders at a house in Portal, made a beeline back to the yard after being moved nearly a mile away. I wonder how many species were on its life list.

Translocating rattlesnakes. Which brings up that second possibility for dealing with an unwanted rattlesnake. Translocation has long been accepted as a humane method of permanently removing an unwanted snake. The Tucson Rural Metro Fire Department and other departments translocate thousands of snakes (and Gila monsters) every year. I've moved more snakes than I can possibly recall for friends and neighbors and people who "got my name from someone." I always assumed that a rattlesnake, with its innate hunting skills and the ability to go long periods without food, would have no trouble adapting to a new environment. Even given the knowledge that I was subtly altering a population balance by adding to the rattlesnake density where I released my captives, I figured it was surely better than just killing the snake.

Unfortunately, the more we learn about rattlesnakes (and other snakes and other animals, as well), the less humane translocation appears to be.

From the moment a rattlesnake is born (rattlesnakes are born, not hatched), it begins learning about its surroundings and incorporating them into a mental map of what will eventually become its territory. As it grows, it probably memorizes thousands of details about terrain, hiding places, food sources, and so forth. This information is vital to the snake's survival, just as your knowledge of your world is to you. If you remove the snake from these familiar surroundings and drop it into a strange environment, there is evidence that its chances for survival plunge—just as yours would if you were dropped into a strange land where you didn't know the language, didn't have money, and had no one to help you. What appears to happen with rattlesnakes, as inferred from radiotelemetry data, is that they immediately begin a single-minded search for familiar landmarks, exposing themselves to predation and slow starvation. (And there is no reason to think this doesn't apply to other animals as well.)

The jury is still somewhat out on translocation, until more studies provide further information on survival rates of translocated snakes. But it's already obvious that it isn't the panacea we once thought it was, and many herpetologists now bluntly offer one piece of advice to homeowners with a resident snake of any kind: "Leave it alone or kill it." Right now, the best compromise if you're going to move a snake seems to be to not move it far—probably less than a half mile—so it has a better chance of winding up in familiar territory. The Drexel Heights Fire Department, for one, has begun incorporating this philosophy into its translocation program. Of course, the closer you release it to your home, the better the chances of it showing up again.

The last resort. For decades, all the above arguments would have been non-sense. If you saw a rattlesnake near your house, you killed it. End of prob-lem. When my family moved from downtown Tucson to a house in the desert in the early 1960s, my stepfather took the shovel to every rattlesnake he saw. The first rattlesnake I killed by myself, when I was eight, seemed like a rite of passage, the detached rattle on my desk a trophy. Not until my teens did I begin to question the morality and necessity of killing rattlesnakes. The first one I captured in our driveway and released unharmed gave me infinitely more pleasure than that first kill. The first one I kept alive in my bedroom, under my stepfather's nose, was even better. He even missed it when he found my Che Guevara poster.

Nevertheless, under certain circumstances it might be necessary for a homeowner to kill a rattlesnake. One that returns repeatedly, even after being translocated a short distance, to a yard where there are small children or pets, has probably proven itself to be a real hazard. At this point your choice is to translocate it miles away and hope for the best, or just dispose of it. Rattlesnakes are rather pathetically easy to kill with the blade of a hoe or shovel (or, of course, a shotgun), but be warned that it is messy and not pleasant. Also, remember that the severed head of a rattlesnake is quite capable of dealing a dangerous bite for several hours. Use a shovel or tongs to pick up the corpse and dispose of it safely. Finally, know that you must possess a valid hunting license to legally kill a rattlesnake in Arizona.

Minimizing problems. If you make the commitment to try to coexist with the rattlesnakes on your property, there are several steps you can take to mini-mize trouble:

1. Maintain wide, clean, and well-lit pathways along your normal routes to your car, outbuildings, and outdoor entertainment areas.
2. Do everything possible to minimize rodent activity near the house.
3. Keep lawns mowed and brush trimmed clear of ground.
4. Watch where you walk! Especially when first stepping out of the house. This rule is so ingrained that I *always* look down when leaving a building, even if it's a Starbucks in downtown Seattle. Another fac-tor here is your choice of footwear. Obviously sandals are more prob-lematic than shoes.
5. Always use a flashlight in dark areas or when hiking at night.

Rattlesnakes and pets. Interestingly, and reassuringly, both cats and dogs usually survive rattlesnake bites, often without any treatment. Cats, if anything, seem to be even better able to survive a bite. Dogs seem to get bitten much more frequently, probably due to their relative lack of caution when exploring (and the fact that a lot more dogs than cats get taken on long hikes through the desert).

If you see your pet get bitten by a rattlesnake, or it shows signs of having been (swelling, extreme sensitivity to touch in the area), get the animal to a veterinarian immediately. He or she will probably give you the option of treating the bite with antivenin, which is very effective and very expensive, or just monitoring the animal and administering IV fluids to help prevent kidney damage.

Unfortunately, with the advent of the new, and much safer for human use, Crofab antivenin, the older horse serum product, which sufficed quite well for pets, has been discontinued. Since the new antivenin seems to be in perpetually short supply, there may come a time soon when antivenin won't even be available for pets, unless veterinarians can source a supply from Mexico or another country.

You can find individuals who will "snake-proof" your dog, using a harmless, but painful, shock collar and a real, but decommissioned, rattlesnake. I've heard this works, but I wonder about the treatment of the snake. Some handlers apparently just yank the fangs out of the snake's mouth. This is obviously stressful to the snake, but also risky, since rattlesnakes have several backup sets of fangs that move into position to take the place of lost ones. Other handlers have the venom glands surgically removed, which might be a safer solution for your dog but also permanently removes the snake's means of capturing prey (the venom also helps in digestion). Then too, a lot of dogs get bitten without ever seeing the snake or hearing it rattle, when they stick their heads into a bush or under-neath something. That's how our border collie got it—training wouldn't have helped a bit (he survived with a stylish scar on his nose). If you'd like to try this approach anyway, I can suggest an alternative that's also a great party trick. Get hold of a rattlesnake rattle and tape it to the end of an electric toothbrush (the kind that wiggles back and forth, not the rotating kind). The noise is amazingly convincing. You can rent a shock collar, or just set the rattle off near the dog and use some other deterrent. Your dog will never go near an electric toothbrush again.

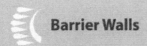
Barrier Walls

One of the best ways to avoid unplanned encounters with snakes is to enclose a space they can't easily get into. A barrier wall surrounding a patio or play area is an effective way to engineer a snake-free area. It will also keep out javelina, Gila monsters, and many other animals you might wish to exclude from at least part of your property.

A barrier wall is nothing more than an ordinary patio wall with a few extra features incorporated to keep snakes out. It doesn't have to be tall—most southwestern snakes are not inclined to try to climb vertical surfaces unless they feel trapped. A three-foot-high wall is sufficient, and low enough not to obscure any views. It needs to be a proper masonry wall on a foundation, however—it's nearly impossible to make a wood fence snake-proof, although Craig Ivanyi says that quarter-inch hardware cloth with the base well buried works quite well. The next step is to ensure that all openings through the wall are snake-proof as well. Storm drains at ground level should be covered at both ends with hardware cloth. And an ordinary gate won't do. You'll need a tightly fitting gate or door that leaves no gaps over a quarter-inch wide on the sides or bottom. You can sometimes modify an existing gate effectively by riveting or screwing strips of stiff rubber to the edges to seal the gaps yet allow the gate to be opened and closed easily.

If you feed birds, you can do so inside the barrier so birds feeding on spilled seed won't attract rattlesnakes, and the seed itself won't attract javelina.

The only downside to barrier walls is psychological: There's a danger one could develop a Maginot mentality, thinking that all those nasty animals are being kept *out there* while you're safe *in here*.

Handling, Capturing, and Moving Snakes

If you've decided to relocate a snake on your own, or you find a snake inside your house and just want to move it outside, you need a method to capture and contain it safely (for both you and the snake). The best method will depend on the size of the snake, and of course whether or not it is venomous. Implements can range from whatever-you-can-grab garden accessories to professional herpetologist tools.

Keep in mind that I cannot possibly recommend that you even get close to a venomous snake, much less manipulate it. The following techniques, then, should be considered suitable for all nonvenomous snakes, and I'll simply tell you which ones are used by experienced handlers for venomous species.

Makeshift tools: The broom and garbage can method. With a broom (a regular witch's broom, not a push broom) and a garbage can laid on its side (or any facsimile thereof), it's *sometimes* possible to maneuver slow-moving snakes into the can, which is then tipped up to trap the snake. The security of the prison, of course, depends inversely on the height of the can and the length of the snake. I had a diamondback rattlesnake that couldn't have been over three feet, six inches long disappear out of a three-foot-tall metal garbage can when I left for ten minutes. That must have been one heck of a tail-stand. So the can should be taller than the snake is long, and even then you should always put the lid on it. Don't worry about suffocating the snake: Like most reptiles, the oxygen needs of a snake are extremely low. A large snake could survive hours and hours on the air inside a garbage can. However, do be cautious about temperature. Do not leave the can in the sun, even if the air temperature is very low. Once you have moved the can to your release site, simply remove the lid by lifting it toward you, then tip the can slowly to the ground *away* from you.

Nooses. Aside from the classic, and utterly useless, forked stick, a noose is what most people call to mind when they think of a tool for capturing snakes. But I don't like nooses, and no herpetologist I've ever spoken to does either. First, they are very hard on the snake. While it's doubtful you could choke a snake with one (remember, snakes can breathe while swallowing something larger than their heads), you could injure it in other ways, by breaking ribs or causing other internal damage. And, in my own experience, snakes seem to react very strongly to nooses, thrashing and twisting as if their instincts recognize the encircling constriction as something really bad. And nooses have the nasty habit of jamming, in which case you have to get to very close proximity with the snake's head to pull the cord loose. There are much better alternatives.

Snake hooks and tongs. A snake hook is a simple tool comprising a handle and shaft with a recurved, blunt hook at the end. Hooks are excellent for maneuvering snakes, pulling them out from under things or, if it's absolutely necessary (which it rarely is, and should *never* be for you), pinning their heads to pick them up by hand. The biggest advantage to a hook is that, if you move slowly, the snake often will not react with alarm, as it never feels constrained. I have at times manipulated rattlesnakes extensively without even eliciting a rattle. But I don't recommend picking up snakes with a hook unless you're an experienced herpetologist, as they can easily slide off. And even just manipulating them takes practice. But a hook is probably the tool least likely to stress the animal.

Tongs, on the other hand, are much easier and more secure to use. A squeeze grip at the handle operates a pair of blunt jaws that can gently grip a snake's body and keep it from sliding or twisting free. The leverage is such that it would be difficult to injure the snake by squeezing too hard. With tongs there's never a need to touch the snake with your hands, yet you can comfortably pick it up to move it a short distance or put it in a garbage can, bag, or other container.

I've seen some nice homemade tongs, but, unless you're quite a machinist, it's much simpler to buy a professional model, available in aluminum for around seventy dollars, or a composite nylon material for a little less. The standard length is around forty inches, which might feel a bit short for those not used to handling snakes, but the longer sizes are awkward and make the snake feel much heavier. The proper technique for lifting a snake with tongs is to gently slide the lower jaw under the snake's body, roughly one-third the length of the body back from the head, then squeeze gently but firmly and lift it off the ground. Done this way, the weight of the snake is properly

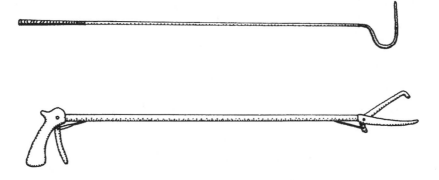

Professional snake-handling tools: (top) a snake hook; (bottom) tongs.

The author uses a snake hook to remove a black-tailed rattlesnake.

supported, but your hands are safely out of reach of its mouth. Be careful not to slide your support hand too far down the shaft. I've found that if I move slowly, the snake often remains very calm during the entire procedure, unless it was agitated to begin with.

Tongs work on Gila monsters too, in the extremely unlikely event you need to move one out of a building (otherwise, they shouldn't be touched). In short, I think snake tongs are the single most useful tool for those who might ever have to move a snake. A seventy-dollar investment is small compared to what that house in the desert cost you.

Many professional herpetologists use snake bags to contain snakes. But it takes practice to maneuver a snake into one, even the type that fits over a rigid frame. And trying it with a venomous snake could be disastrous unless you know exactly what you're doing. A garbage can or similar container, while not as stylish, works just fine.

Capturing snakes inside the house. It's very rare to find large snakes inside a house unless you're in the habit of leaving all the doors open. But small snakes are a different matter, since they can slide beneath many security or screen doors. Most snakes I've found inside houses are less than twenty inches long. And I've found a lot of them, usually at a neighbor's after getting a phone call that sounded something like "GETOVERHERERIGHT NOWTHERE'SAHUGESNAKECRAWLINGTHROUGHMYHOUSEPLEASE HURRYAAAAHHHEREITCOMES!!!!"

If you try to catch one of these snakes, it will no doubt start squirming frantically to get away. On linoleum floors this results in a hilarious lack of actual forward movement for all the thrashing, although on carpet the traction and resulting velocity is much higher.

The easiest way to catch a small nonvenomous snake in the house is by putting a snake bag or an ordinary pillowcase over your hand and arm and using it as an oversized glove to grab the snake firmly but gently. Even if it tries to bite it can't get through the fabric, and you can then simply invert the bag over the snake and tie it off to carry outside.

The only problem with this method is that, unless you have the bag directly at hand, the snake is likely to disappear by the time you get back from the linen closet. The alternative is to simply grab the snake with your bare hands. Sometimes, by putting your hand flat on top of the snake's head, you can then grasp it behind the head to avoid being bitten. However, if you're not squeamish about such things, I can tell you that a bite from a small snake is nothing to worry about. Many of them can't even break the skin with their miniscule teeth, and at most might draw a little blood. And many individuals won't even attempt to bite (although many others adopt the even more effective strategy of wiping the contents of their cloaca all over your hands).

Snake traps and repellents. There might come a time when you need to capture a large or venomous snake, but either don't want to or can't use tongs or another technique. Perhaps the snake has shown up in a cluttered storeroom or garage and you can't get to it, or you just don't fancy wrestling directly with a snake. An attractive solution would be a trap that immobilizes the snake and allows you to move it elsewhere. And such a product is, in fact, on the market.

The trap is a cardboard box about fifteen by thirty inches, but only a couple inches tall, open at both ends. Inside is a chevron-shaped strip of an *extremely* sticky glue. The trap is designed to be placed next to a wall, which is where snakes tend to stay inside a building rather than crawling across the middle of the floor. Since the snake can see through the box it doesn't hesitate to crawl through it, and when it does it is captured by the adhesive. It sounds ludicrous, but the video produced by the company shows a heavy rattlesnake so stuck that the designer opens the box, picks it up and shakes it, while the poor snake just hangs there immobilized, looking most discomfited.

Once you've captured the snake, the instructions say to carry the box to where you want to release the snake, open it, and pour a liberal amount of cooking oil over the adhesive. The snake will supposedly be able to free itself within about thirty minutes.

I must admit to being attracted to the idea of this product as a tool for homeowners, and even ordered a couple for inspection. I couldn't find anything wrong with the theory, except that it was apparent many other animals could also become trapped in the adhesive. I could imagine an inquisitive cactus wren becoming hopelessly mired, probably with fatal results. Nevertheless, the idea seemed to have promise.

But I subsequently received strong condemnations of the glue trap concept from Craig Ivanyi at the Desert Museum, as well as from Janice Bowers, who works at the University of Arizona's Tumamoc Hill laboratory. Craig believes glue traps are quite likely to injure the snake, and Janice told me that when glue traps were tried in the Tumamoc Hill outbuildings the "bycatch" of birds and other nontarget animals was horrible. So it appears we'll have to wait for a more effective and safe invention.

Another product available to homeowners is snake repellent. That's right—a line of this powdered stuff sprinkled along the ground is purported to stop snakes in their, well, tracks. Composed mostly of naphthalene and sulphur, it is purportedly irritating to a snake's highly sensitive olfactory system.

After buying a box of the product (I won't mention the brand because my test was extremely unscientific), I set about testing it. What I wanted was a wild snake that wasn't agitated, but just cruising along. I came across the perfect subject one summer morning: a diamondback rattlesnake winding its way slowly through the desert. I carefully got ahead of its path, without letting it see me, and laid a generous line of repellent on the ground. The snake slowly changed directions, missing the trap altogether. I tried again, and this time it crawled right up to the line, appeared to hesitate a moment— then turned aside. Wow. I got ahead of it again and poured another line. This time it hesitated again, but then crawled across. Hmm. Was the first course change just happenstance?

I called a herpetologist friend to ask about snake repellent, and he called *his* herpetologist friend, who said he had some of the same stuff on trial, and that two or three of his captive snakes were "sleeping in piles of it." Hmm. And Craig Ivanyi confirmed that he had heard of no clinical tests indicating any effectiveness of the product, in addition to which he questioned the wisdom of scattering such potent chemicals around the yard. So, again, the sensational-sounding cure-all falls short of expectations. For now I suggest you stick to the tried-and-true methods we already covered for dealing with uninvited snakes.

Gila Monsters

Despite their fearsome name, the danger posed by Gila monsters near your home—or anywhere else—is so remote as to render statistics meaningless. First, the chances of seeing one are slight: They are extremely secretive, and spend over 90 percent of their lives underground. Gila monsters are nonaggressive and will always attempt to escape if discovered. They are also very sluggish, with the *notable* exception of movements within their own body length, which can be remarkably quick. "Watch this, hon—this thing's movin' so slow I bet I can grab its taiOWW!" In other words, leave them alone and they'll leave you alone. Gila monsters are also protected by law, so it is illegal to kill or capture them.

The Gila monster *(Heloderma suspectum)* is one of only two venomous lizards in the world, the other being the closely related, but larger, Mexican beaded lizard *(H. horridum)* found south of the U.S.–Mexico border. The Gila monster's venom apparatus is sometimes referred to as "primitive," since the venom is delivered through simple grooves in the lower teeth, and the lizard must hang on to its victim and bite down repeatedly to deliver a significant amount. In fact, the venom seems to be unneeded for many of the lizard's normal prey items, such as bird eggs, baby birds, and small mammals, which are simply swallowed whole—although there might be a digestive factor, as there is in rattlesnake venom.

A human clumsy or stupid enough to be bitten is in for a very painful few days, but that's about it. It is remotely possible that a small child or a very frail adult could die from a Gila monster bite; however, in their 1991 book *Gila Monster: Facts and Folklore of America's Aztec Lizard,* authors David

Gila monsters are beautiful and fascinating lizards. They are protected by law and should be left strictly alone.

Gila monsters are slow, and thus prey on things that can't move very quickly—such as these quail eggs. This is why quail lay lots of eggs!

Brown and Neil Carmony were unable to document a single death from a Gila monster bite.

Pets also appear to be in little danger. I had a beagle when I was young that was bitten on the lower lip by a Gila monster. The dog's face swelled somewhat, but she recovered quickly.

8

Small Mammals

Woodrats

Many urbanites who move for the first time into houses surrounded by desert have visions of battling rattlesnakes and scorpions. But they soon find out who their real adversary is: the white-throated woodrat, *Neotoma albigula* (or, as many of us still prefer to call it, the pack rat).

Woodrats are famous for their dens, which, in the wild, are usually located in clumps of prickly pear, under shrubs or trees, or in crevices or small caves. The structures are often-massive accretions of cactus segments, branches and twigs, and all sorts of odds and ends gathered during the rodents' nocturnal foraging, the result being a thorny fortress resistant to attacks from coyotes and other predators, and offering some insulation from temperature extremes as well. If you examine a woodrat den—some of which exceed six feet in diameter and two feet in height—you'll find several entrances that lead to a nest chamber lined with fur and soft plant material. But woodrats are solitary animals except for females with young, so each nest you see houses only one. The extra entrances are really extra *exits*, in case a snake investigates one of them.

Woodrat dens are often used by successive generations of rats, and some have proved to be astonishingly revealing archaeological tools: Thomas Van Devender, Julio Betancourt, and other scientists, investigating middens in caves in Arizona dating back many thousands of years, have been able to reconstruct past plant communities by identifying seeds and other material

Woodrats can squeeze through openings as narrow as one inch wide.

preserved within a multilayered matrix of compacted rat debris and excreta. There, amid the cactus and desert scrub now surrounding these ancient nests, they found parts of oaks and junipers, confirming previous evidence that the Southwest was much cooler ten thousand years ago (they have in fact dated middens as old as fifty thousand years).

The colloquial name *pack rat* comes from the woodrat's propensity for adorning its nest with anything of interest it finds and can carry, including human jetsam: string, shotgun shells, old Bic lighters, six-pack retainers, tin cans, you name it. The most amusing example I know of involved a Captain Roberts, stationed at Fort Bowie in the 1880s, who reported that a pack rat had made off with his front false teeth. The teeth were discovered one hundred years later when the ruins were being cleared. You can see them today at the visitors' center.

Western lore insists that pack rats, when they find something of value to make off with within someone's home, such as a piece of jewelry or silverware, always leave something in its place (leading to yet another folk name for them: *trade rat*). This quid pro quo actually happens on occasion, although biologists suggest that the animal merely drops whatever it's carrying when something shinier catches its eye. But what do scientists know about rodent ethics?

What we do know is that woodrats seem to *love* the proximity of humans. They will gleefully spurn their natural nest sites and build instead in wood piles, brick piles, abandoned cars, crawl spaces, and storerooms. Without doubt the most stylish woodrat nest I've ever seen was fastidiously constructed inside the engine and passenger compartment of a vintage Porsche

356, parked next to the owner's house near Portal, awaiting restoration. I'm convinced this rat was the envy of the neighborhood, albeit probably the target of snide references from his less-successful peers: "Oh, *you* know—the one who lives in the *Porsche*."

Once a woodrat takes up residence in or near your own residence, the hunt is on for treasure, snacks, and just stuff to chew. And there is no rodent on earth with a greater talent for decommissioning mankind's works than *Neotoma albigula*. They seem to be possessed by some sort of fanatic Luddite ethos. Electricity annoys them, and they'll chew through wiring insulation in a pattern guaranteed to short every circuit in the house. They're scornful of indoor plumbing as well, at least the plastic kind, and love to gnaw holes in supply lines. But their most vilified enemy is certainly the internal combustion engine, in any form. A gas-powered lawn mower will do nicely as an apprenticeship, to familiarize the rat with the basics of ignition and fuel interruption. Then it's on to the looming inhabitant of the carport. They'll chew through gasoline lines, wiring, or hoses as the mood takes them, often with the fiendish result that the vehicle will actually start and run perfectly for about a mile before dying in the middle of a crowded intersection. By this time in the sequence of sabotage our mild-mannered, PETA-donating homeowner has progressed from buying Havahart traps to searching the web for military surplus flamethrowers.

The simplest way to prevent woodrat mayhem is to make your house unattractive or unavailable to woodrats. Call it the Martha Stewart Defense: Since woodrats like clutter, *organize*.

In the yard, woodrats look for piles of stuff that contain voids, inside which they can build nest chambers, while covering the exterior in cactus armor. A haphazard jumble of lumber, firewood, or bricks is a perfect foundation; if it's neatly and tightly stacked it won't be as attractive. Better, of course, is to not have such piles at all, or, in the case of lumber, to elevate it well off the ground.

If you have outbuildings for storage, or workshops, build them on a concrete foundation, and make sure the walls and doors fit tightly. Woodrats can squeeze through a slot as little as one inch high. The same caution applies to outdoor cabinets that sit on the ground or a slab. If the doors are wood and there is a slight gap, they'll chew an enlargement. A metal threshold and a metal strip along the bottom of the door will prevent this. Woodrats have no magic powers, despite what your neighbors might tell you—they need some sort of a significant opening to get inside a building.

Find and seal *all* the openings (*most* won't do it!) and you'll seal out the rats.

Once pack rats have found and used a hole, they're much more likely to try to force entrance there if they suddenly find it blocked. So materials such as caulk or expanding foam aren't as effective as sheet metal strips or cement. If you need to exclude rats from vent openings where air circulation must be maintained, use hardware cloth or expanded metal lathe.

If you're lucky enough to have a garage with a tight-fitting door, your vehicles should be relatively safe. Just keep an eye out in your rearview mirror when you come home for little ninja woodrats dashing in under the open door.

If the vehicles must be parked outside or in an open carport, you have a much greater potential for problems. One way to mitigate engine compartment damage is to leave the hood open. Woodrats prefer enclosed places for exploration and building. Remember, though, that sun exposure to soft engine compartment parts can be just as damaging as rodent teeth. Rather than propping the hood wide open on its strut, use a shorter stick to let in light while shading the rubber parts from direct light. A friend of Steve Phillips, publications director at the Desert Museum, uses a shortened broomstick with crutch tips on both ends so it won't slip—an excellent idea.

Another tactic, or actually an additional one, is to park the car in a different place each night. One night at your house, the next night at your aunt's . . . just kidding. What I mean is, simply moving it around in your driveway or, if you have a carport, just swapping ends each time you park. The animals' natural caution keeps them away from things they perceive as novel, especially for nest building, and this movement can throw them off enough to keep them away.

Another possibility for deterring woodrats is a repellent such as naphthalene, the ingredient in mothballs. I've been trying this at my mother's house but haven't reached any firm conclusions yet. No one I could find knows of any controlled tests that have proven the theory. But Kim Duffek, a horticulturalist at the Desert Museum, reports that the mothballs she put out to deter woodrats *disappeared* over several nights. She quipped that the woodrats "probably moved them to their nests to deter kissing bugs" (a common parasite of woodrats).

Incidentally, the most incredible woodrat den I ever dealt with took up an entire tin shed in the backyard of a guest ranch my wife and I were managing. The previous owners had filled the shed with thousands of cast-off plumbing pieces, electrical parts, small appliances, car parts, and lumber. The woodrat that discovered it must have fainted in ecstasy. When I encountered it, the den was wall to wall and waist high, a fantastic farrago of cactus, mesquite, and junk. It was the Hearst Castle of woodrat dens. I was actually nervous while wading through it, fearing that at any moment I might break through to some preternaturally huge central nest chamber and be confronted by an enormous, irate woodrat wearing a smoking jacket.

Rock Squirrels

One morning I sat on the porch, watching a bunch of grosbeaks and cardinals eating seed on a platform feeder in the yard. The feeder was mounted on a four-foot-tall steel tube, high enough to keep it away from the rock squirrels that were common in the canyon. They got the overspill that fell to the ground but would often sit up and gaze at the feeder longingly, like I do at an uncut cake my wife is saving for company.

Except for one of them. This male was the MacGyver of rock squirrels, always trying to figure out a way on to that feeder. He had climbed the mesquite tree near it a dozen times, measuring distances and angles. He tested the pole daily, hoping for an increase in its coefficient of friction. It wouldn't have surprised me to see him drag a branch over and try to tip it up against the edge.

This morning he spied a new possibility. We had repositioned a water trough, and one of the boulders that ringed it was now only a few feet from the base of the pole. It was a fifteen-inch addition to the local elevation, and it didn't escape the calculating eye of MacGyver. He was on it in a flash, squinting at the platform above him like a high jumper eyeing a new record attempt. As I watched, and a couple of female rock squirrels looked on breathlessly, he gathered his legs underneath him and made a mighty leap . . .

And didn't make it. He sailed just under the platform and hit the pole, sliding slowly earthward with all four limbs wrapped around it like a rodentine firefighter. The lady squirrels and I dissolved in hysterics.

Rock squirrels look like a desertified version of a tree squirrel: about the same size and shape, but sort of a mottled dirt-rock color, with a less bushy tail. Actually, as you might infer from their name, rock squirrels are a species of ground squirrel *(Spermophilus variegatus)*. Instead of nesting in hollow trees they dig extensive burrows, often among boulders, which makes it nearly impossible for a large predator to unearth them.

Rock squirrels eat a wide variety of seeds, nuts, fruits, and buds—along with the odd baby bird. They'll happily raid any kind of bird food you put out. Fortunately, as we have seen, they aren't that hard to foil and are otherwise quite amusing to have around.

But be warned: When just one or two rock squirrels show up and begin their antics, one might be tempted to think, "Oh, how cute," and give them some extra food. Take my advice and let them make their own living, because under favorable conditions they can breed like the Andromeda Strain, and you could find yourself in a Hitchcock-esque nightmare of rock squirrels, searching the yellow pages fruitlessly for Rent-a-Bobcat. A single hole and a small mound of dirt will morph into a subterranean warren with something resembling the tailings pile of a strip mine engulfing half the yard.

To keep rock squirrels off your seed feeders, just mount them on metal poles at least four feet tall, and away from overhanging trees or other climbable objects. And don't leave any Swiss Army knives or other multitools where they can find and use them. I've also found that they can be dissuaded from excavating in the yard *if* you catch them at it early. I did with one pair, and simply began filling their incipient holes with water and then putting big rocks over them. They soon moved elsewhere, no harm done. But you'll need to be vigilant for this to work—once the tunnels are complete, they're almost impossible to destroy completely.

Totally Urban Wildlife: The House Mouse

The urban areas of Arizona have been thoroughly colonized by the ubiquitous house mouse *(Mus musculus)*, found virtually worldwide wherever there are humans, including oceanic islands. A member of the Old World subfamily of rats and mice, Murinae, the house mouse probably originated in the Mediterranean region before hitching its fortune, with fabulous success, to that of *Homo sapiens.*

A house mouse can be nearly impossible to distinguish from certain wild mice, such as many members of the genus *Peromyscus:* cactus mice, deer mice, and others. House mice have nearly hairless tails, but that's hard to see unless you're holding one.

However, house mice are almost completely tied to human habitation

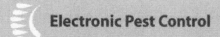

Electronic Pest Control

You can't help but be tempted by a product that promises to chase away rodents forever without harming them. There are a whole bunch of such devices on the market, some of which use ultrasound (that is, noise above the range of human hearing), and others that claim to use your home's existing wiring to produce an annoying (to rodents) electromagnetic field throughout your entire house, simply by plugging the product into any outlet. The ads for each type promise miracles. Unfortunately, the evidence for the effectiveness of such products is virtually nil.

Controlled tests of ultrasound generators inside buildings reveal that, indeed, some small rodents such as mice initially move away from the source of the sound. However, they invariably become accustomed to the noise, return, and go back to their normal activities. Tests conducted outdoors revealed even less effect on pocket gophers and other burrowing rodents.

As far as the "electromagnetic field generators" are concerned, well, the testers whose reports I read could barely conceal their collective derision. Suffice to say that to do what their proponents claim, such devices would have to violate several laws of electromagnetism. Save your money.

(they also colonize cultivated fields). If you live within the city and have mice in your house or garage, they are almost certainly house mice.

There's almost no health danger from house mice, unlike their larger European rat relatives, but they can cause damage to structures and possessions as they build nests and forage for food (which is anything you or your pet will eat, plus your soap, glue, and many other household compounds).

Pocket Gophers

If you find small piles of fresh dirt in your yard, a foot or so in diameter, with an obvious dirt plug where it appears an entrance should be, you have pocket gophers.

Several species of pocket gopher occur in Arizona, but one is far more widespread than the rest: Botta's pocket gopher (*Thomomys bottae*).

Pocket gophers live nearly their entire lives underground, coming to the surface to push out dirt from their tunnels, then plugging the entrance. They

The Final Rodent Solution: Poison versus Traps

A pest control technician once described to me, with a perfectly straight face, the process by which a woodrat would succumb to his company's rodenticide: "They just lie down and go to sleep and don't wake up."

He was probably simply repeating what the poison manufacturer told him, but I'm afraid I don't share his cheerful assurance.

While it may horrify some people, under certain circumstances there might be no reasonable alternative to a lethal solution to a rodent problem. Done judiciously, there are no ecological consequences—the rodents in question are hardly endangered; in fact, it's quite likely the homeowner will find himself back where he started just weeks after indulging in an orgy of furry murder. Nevertheless, if you decide to remove some rodent residents permanently, you'll want to do it as responsibly and humanely as possible. But, while pest control companies might try to assure you that poison is a suitable approach, there is considerable evidence to the contrary.

The two most commonly administered classes of rodenticide, courmarins and indandiones, both achieve their ends by blocking the formation of a vitamin-K dependent substance called prothrombin, which is an essential element in blood clotting. In other words, these poisons act as powerful anticoagulants. One of the courmarins, warfarin, is commonly administered therapeutically in humans, to prevent blood clotting after certain operations. But when used in concentrated form as a rodenticide, its effects on the animal begin with bleeding from the nose and gums, blood in the urine and feces, bruises and skin damage from ruptured blood vessels, and cerebral hemorrhaging. The animal usually dies within two days to a couple of weeks after ingesting a fatal dose. Doesn't sound very peaceful to me.

If that were the end of it, things would be bad enough, Unfortunately, courmarins and indandiones do not degrade when ingested, and can affect a predator that eats the poisoned rodent. Since a target animal can wander a good distance after ingesting the poison, and in an increasingly weakened state, the chances of it being grabbed by a coyote or bobcat or hawk obviously skyrocket. When the World Health Organization issued its report on these rodenticides in 1998, secondary poisoning had been demonstrated in the laboratory but had not been reported in the wild. That is no longer the case: The Southwest Wildlife Rehabilitation and Education Center has documented warfarin poisoning in coyotes, bobcats, javelina, ringtails, foxes, and several raptors. Since the only treatment is an intensive, multiday program of vitamin K injections (which must be started *before* the animal is sick enough to display symptoms and allow itself to be captured), these animals are doomed. Not a ringing endorsement of poison as a responsible rodent-control device.

A lot of people—even those who willingly employ poison—abhor the idea of using snap traps to kill mice and rats, supposedly on humane grounds, but I suspect a good part of their reluctance is self-centered. Using a snap trap means direct involvement: You have to see the poor little thing you've killed and deal with its remains. With poison you can sort of ignore the whole arrangement and hope the target wanders away and "goes to sleep" somewhere else. (Instead, you often wind up with a putrefying corpse wedged in the back of the storeroom or inside a wall.)

Snap traps are actually extremely humane. The animal is typically either killed instantly, or else it escapes unharmed. And if you want to anthropomorphize, the last thought in its tiny brain is a happy one: *"Cool, look at this big, big piece of peanut butter someone forg—"*

The ancient little wood-based Victor mouse trap (and no, no one has yet invented a better one) comes in both mouse and rat sizes and is easily set and baited with a bit of peanut butter dabbed on the trigger, the stickiness of which makes it more likely the animal will trip the release. It's best placed along a wall in the space where you've been having problems, since mice stick close to cover. If cost isn't a concern and you're squeamish about corpses you can throw the whole thing away when it's caught something. Snap traps can't injure pets or children.

But remember the axiom stated earlier: If you just kill the rodent and do nothing to alter what attracted it and allowed it access, you're certain to experience the same problem soon.

If you simply can't stand the thought of killing something, you could try relocation. And of course if you've just made a building rodent-proof and simply need to move the current, now-walled-in residents outside, a live trap makes perfect sense. Victor and other companies also make live mouse traps that can hold from a few to a dozen or more. These have transparent covers so you can easily check them, and sliding hatches to release the mice. Other companies, such as Tomahawk and Sherman, manufacture metal box traps suitable for woodrats. The Sherman folding box traps are easy to use and effective, and take up very little space when stored.

I could find no evidence as to the survival rate of small rodents moved far from their home range and released, but I suspect it is fantastically low. I believe relocating mice or woodrats would serve little purpose except to falsely soothe the conscience of the homeowner. Then again, one could argue that the rodent's fate would most likely be a quick end at the hands of a predator, which would at least serve a useful ecological purpose. And of course you could always release them in the garage of that neighbor of yours who likes to play Black Sabbath CDs and tune his Harley at 2:00 A.M.

are thought to contribute valuable aeration to the soil. Pocket gophers dig with their powerful front claws and also with their incisors, which need to be continually ground down or they would grow as much as fourteen inches per year. They feed on plants, which they often pull straight down into their burrow, exactly like one of those cartoons where the farmer's carrots all disappear one at a time.

Pocket gophers can, indeed, cause real problems for farmers, especially alfalfa growers and those with root crops. Around your home they will do very little damage—unless you have your own garden, which they will gleefully appropriate. There is very little you can do to exclude them, short of burying the perimeter fence down to a depth of three feet or so. One person I know does claim to have permanently driven the gophers from his garden by repeatedly flooding their tunnels. The only other approach is the lethal one: Since pocket gophers have a fairly restricted home range (about 2,000 to 2,200 square feet for males, the area of a large house) and appear to be somewhat territorial, it's sometimes possible to trap the resident of the garden and have a gopher-free crop—for a while, anyway.

Other Rodents—and Disease

There are many other species of rodents in southern Arizona: cactus mice, deer mice, several species of pocket mice, grasshopper mice, and kangaroo rats. But most of these seem less inclined to invade human habitation than the ones I've discussed, and only rarely cause any trouble. They're much more likely to be found—in very large numbers indeed—in abandoned buildings, where numerous openings gain them easy entrance. But occasionally one will find its way into a storeroom or other building currently in use. When this has happened to me, a careful search usually turns up the entrance, which is easily blocked. I then put out a live trap, capture the animal, and just let it go outside. Small mice can squeeze through a slot less than three quarters of an inch high, so you need to be thorough.

Many people in the Southwest worry about Hantavirus, a virulent and, indeed, often fatal disease spread by certain species of rodents, chief among them the deer mouse *(Peromyscus maniculatus)*. Actually the disease caused by the virus is called Hantavirus Pulmonary Syndrome, or HPS. It begins with disarmingly typical flulike symptoms, but then progresses rapidly to severe pulmonary edema (fluid buildup in the lungs). There is no vaccine or cure, and the fatality rate is close to 40 percent. Although different strains of Hantaviruses (most of which attack the kidneys, not the lungs) are found worldwide, ours, known as the *Sin Nombre* virus ("No Name" in Spanish), is almost entirely confined to the southwestern states.

That's the bad news. The good news is that since the regional Hantavirus was first identified in 1993, we have learned much about it, including how uncommon it actually is, and how people can avoid infection.

The mice that carry Hantavirus expel it in their urine, feces, and saliva, where it remains viable for several days. People who contract the virus usually do so after stirring up the dust and debris where infected mice live or forage, thus inhaling the pathogen. Many of the victims have been rural residents living in close proximity to mice in poor sanitary conditions. Keep in mind that hundreds of thousands of southwestern residents (especially Native Americans living on reservations) fit this profile, but that fewer than three hundred cases of HPS were reported between 1993 and 2001. It is a very difficult disease to catch.

Nevertheless, you can minimize your already minimal chances with a few simple precautions, mainly by keeping mice out of your living areas. If you have to clean out a building where recent rodent activity is apparent, wear rubber or latex gloves and an EPA-approved respirator (not just a dust mask). If you can seal up the building after excluding the rodents, and wait a few weeks before cleaning it, the chances of encountering any viable virus will be virtually nonexistent. Also note that Hantavirus cases peak with rodent population surges, which frequently occur during or directly after years with heavy rains.

Skunks

They say there are two kinds of dogs who meet their first skunk. The first kind investigates, gets sprayed, and never wants to have anything to do with skunks again. The second kind investigates, gets sprayed—and vows revenge on every single skunk it meets for the rest of its life.

Wouldn't you know I'd have the second kind while I was a kid? I spent so much time up to my elbows in tomato juice lathering that dog that to this day I have never needed a vitamin C supplement.

Poor skunks. They just want to be left alone. No healthy skunk has ever run after a dog or anything else with the intent of spraying it. They only do

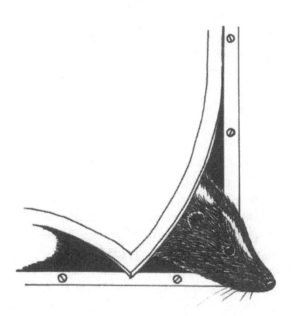

An exciting combination:
a skunk and a pet door.

so as a last resort, after every warning in the book has failed. And their weapon does no lasting damage—it's just, "If you mess with me, I'll make it . . . *unpleasant* for you."

Our region boasts (some people might disagree with that term) all four skunk species found in the United States: striped, spotted, hooded, and hognosed (the last two are found only in the Southwest). All are omnivorous, although the little spotted skunk—which, if you can get over your skunk aversion, is one of the prettiest little animals on earth—is more carnivorous than the rest. All are nocturnal and generally avoid people, unless they have become accustomed to raiding campsites or picnic areas, when they will walk between your legs to get at your food. But since those skunks are acclimated, they are even less likely to spray unless seriously provoked. Like if you won't hand over the potato chips. Just kidding.

One bit of mischief skunks are known for is discovering and using pet doors to snag the contents of a food bowl. The best prevention for this is to feed your pet during the day, then remove the bowl. And block off the pet door at night! Skunks are also attracted to compost piles, so be sure yours is totally enclosed.

Skunks are notorious for being frequent carriers of rabies, and in this case, there is some truth in the folklore. Note that they are not "carriers," that is, skunks die from rabies just like any other mammal. But they are susceptible to spikes in infection rates during rabies outbreaks, probably because their normal defensive apparatus doesn't keep other rabid animals from attacking them. Nevertheless, it is extremely uncommon to discover rabid skunks, and often the local game and fish and health departments are aware of outbreaks and issue alerts so you can be extra cautious. Identifying a potentially rabid skunk is simple: They act like no normal skunk would, including—especially—being out in broad daylight, showing no fear of humans or pets or even being aggressive, and staggering or moving in sudden spurts. If you see a skunk acting this way, leave immediately (or go inside if it's near your house) and call the game and fish department to report it.

Incidentally, while tomato juice still works adequately as skunk odor remover, a more effective solution is one quart of 3 percent hydrogen peroxide mixed with a quarter cup baking soda and a tablespoon of liquid soap. Lather the animal and work the suds in thoroughly, keeping it away from eyes and ears, then rinse extremely thoroughly.

Bats

To get one thing out of the way: Arizona does not have any vampire bats. They occur much farther south. Vampire bats really do consume blood, although it's far less dramatic than the Hollywood approach: They crawl quietly up to a sleeping cow or other large animal (only rarely a human) and gently scrape an incision in the skin with their incisors, then lap the blood that flows. Not much different than a big, furry mosquito.

In spite of an aggressive fact-disseminating campaign by bat experts, many people still think of bats as habitual carriers of rabies. But not only is the presence of rabies in the bat population no higher than in other mammal groups (and lower than some), bats that do contract full-blown rabies die quickly from it, just like any other animal. If some self-proclaimed expert tries to tell you that bats are asymptomatic carriers of rabies (the term for an animal that can harbor a disease without displaying symptoms), tell him he is full of bat guano.

As an aside, the reason I specified "full-blown rabies" above is that some new evidence gathered by bat researcher Tom O'Shea and his colleagues in Fort Collins, Colorado, indicates that bats might have evolved antibodies that protect them from low exposures to the rabies virus. There is still no evidence for any carrier stage, however.

Occasionally a bat or two will find a spot on a house suitable for roosting. I visited a friend once who kept finding what she thought were mouse droppings near her front door. I looked up near the roof and saw a trim board that lay flat against the wall, except for a gap about an inch wide. Shining my flashlight up there, we discovered the source of the droppings: a single bat that had decided this was a great roost. Fortunately, my friend was delighted, and glad to leave the bat its spot until it left several weeks later.

Hopefully, you will be as delighted if you find a resident bat. They typically will leave after a few weeks. If not, or if you find a lot of them, or if they are roosting in a place where you really don't want droppings underneath, it's simplicity itself to exclude them. Just wait one evening until the bats leave to hunt, then fill the cavity with expanding foam sealant, or nail a board of the appropriate width in the gap. Be extremely cautious if you do this during summer, however, as you could have a female bat with young that she leaves in the spot while hunting. Either make darn sure there's nothing in there, or wait until the bat leaves for the winter before blocking the space.

Much more rarely, you might find a bat inside a building simply clinging to a wall, asleep. Capturing it is easy. Just find a coffee can and a piece of thin cardboard wider than the can. Put on a pair of gloves (no bat in Arizona can bite through a normal pair of leather work gloves), and place the open end of the can over the bat. Then slowly slide the cardboard underneath until you dislodge it. Take it outside and gently decant it somewhere warm. Sleeping bats cannot just take off; they need to raise their body temperature first. If you just flung the bat into the air it would almost certainly plunge to the ground, resulting in serious injury.

When I'm faced with a hanging bat needing eviction, I simply grasp it carefully with the gloves and remove it. But if you use this method you need to be extremely cautious, as bats are remarkably fragile, and you could inadvertently break a wing bone.

Even more rarely you might find an obviously sick bat, lying on the ground in the middle of the day. If you don't have the fortitude to put it out of its misery (a fast whack with the flat of a shovel is effective and merciful), you can still move it without touching it, or call a wildlife rehabilitator in case they might be willing to collect it. But don't call a pest control company and let them convince you that you have a "bat problem" and need some sort of expensive treatment. You don't.

For more detailed information about the fascinating world of bats, buy a copy of *America's Neighborhood Bats*, by Merlin D. Tuttle.

Large Mammals

Javelina

At about 2:00 A.M. a few years ago, my wife and I woke up to a familiar sound—the short, snuffling grunts of feeding javelina. This wouldn't have been remarkable in the least, except that we weren't in the remote house we lived in for three years in Brown Canyon, and we weren't in the house we lived in in Cave Creek Canyon, and we weren't even in either of our parents' houses on the outskirts of Tucson. We were in our little in-town house just two blocks south of the University of Arizona football stadium, smack in the middle of urban Tucson. Only a small, natural wash next to us retained a strip of native vegetation and the odd coyote looking for unwary house cats. We crept out to the back gate with a flashlight, and there they were—two javelina, unconcernedly grazing on the birdseed scattered on the ground. They barely registered our presence before going back to feeding.

I was used to stories of bold suburban javelina, but as near as I could tell this was a record for in-town excursions. We never saw them again, but several neighbors who live along Arroyo Chico have reported their own visitors.

Not to be anthropomorphic, but javelina display an attitude toward intrusive housing developments that borders on the pugnacious. I've seen herds of them strolling down freshly paved streets and into yards laid with crisp Bermuda grass sod, with all the assurance and beady-eyed appraisal of nosy neighbors checking out the new people on the block. If a few soft-hearted folks make the mistake of feeding them dog food or kitchen scraps,

Javelina will vacuum birdseed and destroy gardens if not discouraged.

they accept it as their entitlement and raise a ruckus if the offerings stop. Years ago a woman who lived near the Tucson Mountains began feeding javelina nightly, a habit that continued without incident for months until she left on vacation for two weeks and didn't arrange a substitute. The evening she returned she opened her sliding glass door, whereupon about a dozen javelina charged into the house and began disassembling the furniture in a panic once they realized they were trapped, while the woman stood on her kitchen table and screamed into her telephone for the sheriff.

Javelina (*no one* calls them by their proper common name, collared peccary, and you'll brand yourself as a newcomer or a nerd if you do so) are not in the pig family, Suidae, but their own, Tayassuidae, reflecting certain anatomical differences from true pigs, such as the presence of a scent gland just above the tail, fused leg and foot bones, a more complex stomach, and enlarged canines that interlock when closed, resulting in a flat, shearing surface between them. Nevertheless they are obviously piglike, short and stout, with a similar nose useful for rooting in the ground for food. They weigh between thirty-five and forty-five pounds, sometimes a bit more.

Homeowners with javelina trouble should count their blessings: One ancestral peccary species that lived about a million years ago stood three feet high at the shoulder and weighed 125 pounds or more. Imagine a dozen of *those* in the living room.

Javelina are actually recent immigrants to southern Arizona. Before the 1800s there were no records of them north of what is now the U.S. border.

Javelina tend to congregate in small herds of eight to twelve, although solitary males are common too. You can often spot tiny newborns trotting along with the herds, and these juveniles are, in technical biological terms, the cutest damn things you'll ever see. Javelina have no specific breeding season, so babies can show up almost anytime, although there seems to be a peak in summer.

In their normal habitat, which ranges from desert scrub up into oak grasslands, javelina feed heavily on prickly pear cactus and agave, along with roots, mesquite beans, and other vegetation. Surprisingly, they'll also scarf up small items of carrion now and then.

In urban settings, javelina will eat dog and cat food, birdseed, and almost any kind of kitchen garbage. Years ago there was a persistent legend about a herd of outlandishly huge javelina accustomed to gorging on leftovers discarded behind an upscale Italian restaurant on the far west side of Tucson. Supposedly a bow hunter discovered the herd and rather overwhelmingly captured first place in an annual javelina hunting contest several years in a row, until someone discovered the secret of his pasta-augmented success. If it's not true, it should be.

In any case, javelina very quickly become accustomed to being fed, and to the presence of humans. Unfortunately, they can also be extremely aggressive, especially when they have young, and when pets, particularly dogs, are around. There have been several recorded instances of people walking dogs being attacked by javelina, resulting in injuries to both dog and human, and a couple of people have been bitten in their own yards. In every case I have researched, it was clear the javelina were used to people and had been fed by neighbors, if not the actual people involved.

While it is undoubtedly thrilling for people who live at the edge of desert habitat to be able to boast of having javelina in the yard, it is a *bad* situation—for the javelina, the humans, and the pets. A single javelina could easily kill a large dog, or do severe damage to an adult human. Yet even people who have been warned and should know better continue to put out food. I'm not in favor of laws prohibiting such behavior, but I am in favor of massive peer pressure. If you know someone who feeds javelina, get a bunch of your neighbors together and *demand* that they stop. Let them know that they are endangering themselves, the javelina, and you. Nothing is more selfish than a so-called animal lover who persists in behavior that results in a wild animal becoming a hazard, thus often ensuring its destruction.

But javelina don't necessarily need an invitation to show up in your yard. Gardens, lawns, birdseed spilled from feeders, ponds, pets fed outdoors, and many other things might attract them whether you want to or not. Fortunately the solutions are pretty straightforward.

Javelina are good-sized animals, but they aren't very agile or athletic. A three-foot-high patio wall is sufficient to exclude them (see the sidebar on barrier walls). A chain-link or sheep fence the same height and buried at least a foot in the ground will keep them out of gardens. If you can't put in something that extensive, an electric fence consisting of a single wire at a height of around twelve inches is also very effective. Electric fences produce very high voltage but low amperages, and won't injure the animals (or pets or children).

If you're having trouble with invasions in places where physical barriers aren't practical, your only recourse is to make it unpleasant for them to be there. Fortunately, as herd animals, you normally only have to scare off one to make the rest flee as well. I've used firecrackers—which, of course, are illegal in Arizona—and many other loud noises with success (unfortunately, if you have nearby neighbors, the danger here is that *you* will wind up being viewed as the nuisance). An aluminum drink can with a few pebbles or coins in it, shaken vigorously, makes an obnoxious racket. A slingshot works great to get a more painful message across, as does, I hear, pepper spray, but of course you have to get pretty close for either of these to be effective. Some people have reported good luck scattering mothballs on lawns. Of course, an even better approach here is to, *ahem,* rip out the lawn. Whatever you try, persistence will be necessary, because javelina are stubborn little buggers. Once they leave, follow them in your car and find out which of your neighbors is feeding them.

Coyotes

What can I say about the coyote that could pay adequate homage to its survival skills, intelligence, and insouciant scorn of our every attempt to

When javelina feed on prickly pear cactus, the result is this shredded effect.

eradicate it? Oh, and we have tried, beginning with the massive government trapping and poisoning campaigns of the early and mid-twentieth century, which so successfully eradicated the grizzly bear and wolf. According to Donald Hoffmeister in *Mammals of Arizona*, between 1915 and 1945 over one and a half million coyotes were killed by U.S. Fish and Wildlife Service agents alone—an average of fifty thousand per year. In part, these huge numbers were achieved because agents targeted litters, dumping gasoline down den holes and lighting it, or dragging the pups out one by one with fish hooks tied to poles, then stomping them to death.

Astonishingly, this war continues today, mostly through the efforts of another taxpayer-funded organization formerly known as Animal Damage Control, now benignly renamed Wildlife Services. According to Wildlife Service's own tables, in 2000, the latest year for which figures had been released when I investigated, the agency killed 86,955 coyotes, plus 6,063 foxes, 2,555 bobcats, and hundreds of badgers, mountain lions, and black bears. In one year.

Coyote control proponents make the point that if the U.S. coyote population can sustain this kind of culling, and still remain not only viable, but vibrant, it possibly points to a genuine need to control their numbers to avoid the much more tragic situation that results from an overpopulated species. The chief complaint against Wildlife Services is that its work largely benefits a relatively small number of private ranchers and farmers, and appears to be, despite recent attempts at reform, alarmingly indiscriminate in strategy. Thousands of coyotes are shot from helicopters simply for being in an area where sheep or cattle are grazed; more are trapped or poisoned. Opponents of Wildlife Services contend that, if predator control were the financial responsibility of the individual rancher, economics would demand that he or she be considerably more circumspect in targeting animals that actually prey on livestock. They also claim that predation could be drastically reduced through more responsible herding practices, particularly by sequestering lambing ewes and calving cows.

Another powerful argument against massive coyote control efforts hinges on a fascinating tidbit of coyote biology—evidence suggests that when the population is reduced, females respond by simply producing larger litters. Also, the beta female in a family group might produce a litter as well, when normally she would not. So attempting to control coyote numbers by killing them might be, in a very real sense, like dowsing a fire with gasoline.

In any case, the danger of the coyote appearing on the endangered species list is remote. The reaction of *Canis latrans* to a century of persecution has been to *increase* its range, colonizing the eastern states and New Brunswick, pushing north into Arctic Canada and Alaska, to the California coast, and even farther south into Central America. Coyotes happily inserted themselves into niches vacated by the less successful wolves, and exploited new niches created by the proximity of humans. Forays into and even colonization of urban areas by coyotes are commonplace, undoubtedly capped by the bold individual known as Lucky Pierre, who made it into New York City's Central Park in 1999 before being tranquilized and removed (he gained his nickname after being darted near the Pierre Hotel). The Arizona Game and Fish Department estimates that there are around two hundred thousand coyotes in Arizona.

Several years ago in Tucson, my wife and I tracked a coyote that was frequenting a neighborhood south of Glenn and east of Campbell, smack in the middle of town. We finally deduced that this individual was accessing the area through a storm drain that ran underground for over a mile north to the Rillito River. And I'm aware of dozens of similar stories.

Coyotes and Domestic Pets

A large part of the success of the coyote has to be credited to its diet, which can include everything from grasshoppers to elk, plus a variety of plant material such as cactus fruit and mesquite beans. Under normal conditions in the wild, the bulk of the coyote's diet consists of small rodents and Lagomorphs (rabbits and hares), but the menu easily expands when the situation presents itself.

Such as when domestic cats are available.

It's tempting to ascribe some deeper meaning to the alacrity with which coyotes will prey on cats. One could postulate, for example, that for millennia our coyotes have had scant outlet for the natural enmity between canids and felids. They certainly wouldn't challenge a mountain lion or jaguar, and even a bobcat would be a dangerous handful for a twenty-five-pound coyote. Thus a deep, genetic-memory persecution complex was formed, to be offered joyful release when soft, rather stupid, ten-pound felids were suddenly added to the prey base. Of course, such speculation would be silly and extremely unscientific, so I won't even mention it. Besides, coyotes will nab a Persian or a poodle with equal relish, so any idea that it's a canine-vs.-feline thing sort of goes out the window.

But the fact remains, urban coyotes do dine on cats with regularity. One case that made the news in Tucson involved a gentleman newly immigrated from the east coast whose cat, naive to the ways of the Wild West, served itself up as an entree for a pair of coyotes within days of arrival. The cat's owner had the extraordinary impertinence to file a lawsuit against the Arizona Game and Fish Department, asking for damages, and even showed up in court with the cat's ashes in a little urn. Fortunately, the case was tossed out. I thought Game and Fish should have countersued on behalf of the coyotes, claiming loss of habitat due to the gentleman's house, pain and trauma from cat scratches, and possible long-term health effects from the cat's chemically laden diet.

Feeding Coyotes

While small pets are at the most risk from coyotes right now, there is a much more disturbing specter on the horizon: Coyote attacks on humans, once virtually unheard of, are becoming more common. Arizona now records about one or two incidents per year, usually involving a child; California

A coyote looking for ... rabbits? Or stray cats?

experiences roughly the same rate. In 1981, a three-year-old girl was killed by several coyotes in the Los Angeles area—the only death ever recorded from a coyote attack, a fact that could have been but small consolation to the little girl's parents.

Please keep one thing firmly in mind: Even now, attacks on humans by coyotes are vanishingly infrequent. About a dozen people are killed by domestic dogs every year in the United States; compare that to one death by coyotes *ever*, and you'll see why hysteria is not needed here. Nevertheless, human-coyote incidents are becoming regular enough to need addressing.

The reason for the increase is simple: Coyotes living near expanding urban areas are becoming less and less afraid of humans, because humans insist on treating coyotes like cute dogs rather than wild animals. Please reread that sentence carefully.

A coyote that has been fed by humans and readily approaches them is not *tame*. It is simply *accustomed*. If something happens to alarm the animal, it will react defensively out of fear, as its instincts demand. Worse, if the animal becomes so accustomed that it *loses* its fear, it might well react aggressively if it perceives a threat to, say, its food source. Worse still, it might become bold enough to view a small human *as* a food source. This is what seems to happen in many of the incidents involving children.

I'll be blunt: People who feed suburban coyotes might as well be pulling puppies out of den holes and stomping them. Those coyotes are headed for trouble. Or, as many Game and Fish Department officers put it: A fed coyote is a dead coyote.

And the ramifications go far beyond the individual animal someone insists on feeding, which then bites a child who has approached it, and which is then destroyed by government officials. If enough of these incidents pile up, the attitude of all those millions of suburbanites infringing on the edges of coyote habitat is likely to undergo a sea change, and they'll suddenly start demanding that *all* of these "dangerous animals" be removed or killed. That would be a terrible day.

No . . . the best way we can honor coyotes is to treat them as what they are—wild animals that are thrilling to spot now and then in their natural habitat. The kindest thing we can do for coyotes as a species is to ensure they remain healthily apprehensive of all humans.

How to do this? First, don't let coyotes associate humans with food. Whether it involves kitchen scraps tossed over the back fence, pet food left outside, or Fluffy herself left outside, coyotes learn faster than an average eleven-year-old with a new video game. They'll be back for more. Second, while it might go against every Bambified gene in your body, *discourage* any coyote that seems acclimated to humans or allows you to approach it. Yell at it, throw rocks, whatever—you'll be doing that coyote the biggest favor of its life. Third, try to educate any neighbors you know who feed coyotes. But I'll warn you, this might be difficult. People who feed animals in spite of irrefutable evidence that it is harmful can be astonishingly stubborn and self-centered.

If you have dogs or cats, keep them inside at night. If they must be outside, make sure they have a means of escape into a place a coyote is unlikely to venture. I haven't heard of a coyote following a cat through a pet door. Yet. Still, even this approach is risky, since if a coyote is hunting your pet it won't let its presence be known until escape is unlikely.

Coyotes can't get over a standard, six-foot, chain-link fence, so it's simple to provide your dogs a safe area. But domestic cats can get *out* of things that coyotes can't get into, so unless you're willing to build your cats a roofed, completely enclosed yard or play area, they'll be vulnerable. A possible alternative: Two friends of mine who live in the desert and have several cats enclosed a large yard in a chain-link fence with an inward-sloping wire guard at the top. Yeah, it looks a bit like Stalag 17—but they haven't lost any cats yet, either.

If you live near coyote habitat and do nothing to turn them into nuisance animals, you'll enjoy the occasional sight of them, and the nightly chorus of their family groups, with a clear conscience.

Bears

The last Arizona grizzly bear was shot in 1936 in Escudilla by a baited rifle tied to a tree by a government hunter, completing the extirpation in our state of a magnificent species that formerly ranged from the Mogollon Rim south through the Santa Catalina and Rincon Mountains and along the Santa Cruz River. Since then, the only Arizona bear has been *Ursus americanus*, the black bear. Fortunately, they appear to be doing well; by most estimations, the population is more or less stable.

But "more or less stable" in a natural population implies a great deal of flux. Black bears prosper in years of good rains and plentiful food supplies, but because of their relatively large size, they suffer quickly when conditions turn bad. In the oak-juniper and ponderosa woodland habitat black bears prefer here, their chief food source is juniper berries, acorns, piñon nuts, and other fruits and nuts, and production of these shuts down almost totally when seasonal rains fail. The result is a lot of stressed, hungry, and thirsty bears showing up in places they normally don't, such as suburban Tucson and Phoenix—or, quite often, dead alongside the highways leading into those cities. However, once environmental conditions return to normal, the bears also return to their normal habitat.

A much more serious problem results when residents near that normal habitat either deliberately feed bears, or feed birds and other animals with food that also attracts bears. These bears quickly become accustomed to human presence and create a potential for significant property damage and human injury. Several years ago, the Arizona Game and Fish Department cracked down on the residents of Mount Lemmon, north of Tucson, some of whom had long been feeding bears. One woman, who reportedly bought ice cream gallons at a time to feed "her" bears, was rather belligerently uncooperative, in spite of being fined. Shortly after this situation was reported, a sixteen-year-old girl at a scout camp nearby was mauled on the leg and scalp by a bear as she slept. It wasn't the bear's fault, and it wasn't the girl's fault. And it wasn't the Forest Service's fault or that of Arizona Game and Fish, who had previously translocated this bear when it reportedly attacked another young girl, only to have it make its way back. Few would blame them for trying a nonlethal approach to the problem (nevertheless, they were of course sued over the matter). This attack was the fault of those people who had been feeding bears and making them unafraid of humans.

Bears are an occasional nuisance in the little community of Portal, next to the Chiricahua Mountains in southeastern Arizona, where we lived for two years. The residents there nearly all feed birds, especially hummingbirds, and bears love both sugar water and seed. Several years ago the problems peaked when seasonal rains failed and natural food was scarce. After bears damaged a couple of houses breaking in to look for food, a few residents formed an ad hoc committee and suggested ways to discourage them, chief of which was taking in all feeders every night. Several residents religiously adhered to this routine, including our eighty-five-year-old neighbor, Sally Spofford, whose yard was known literally worldwide as a birding haven. Others didn't, and the bears continued raiding yards, until a single resident complained to the Game and Fish Department. The department promptly trapped the bear in question and shot it. We couldn't blame the department; part of their mandate is to protect the public (and, obviously, protect themselves from lawsuits), and a belligerent black bear was, as everyone now knew, a serious hazard. Once again, it was the fault of the few residents too lazy and selfish to change their ways.

Bobcats

Bobcats, a problem? I don't think so. They aren't a danger to humans, they deserve anything they might snatch from your bird feeders, and if they take a neighborhood cat or poodle now and then it's because the pets aren't properly supervised. In fact, the only reason I mentioned them here is so I could pass on a piece of advice I read in a "problem wildlife" pamphlet, an answer to a question from someone who apparently *did* consider bobcats undesirable. The person asked what kind of a fence would keep a bobcat out. The answer, which I strongly suspect was tongue-in-cheek, read: "A bobcat won't jump into something it can't see into. The fence must be made of solid material, not wood, as bobcats can easily climb up wood. A 12-foot-tall solid fence topped with wire on poles should do the trick."

Yup. Just the ticket for you bobcat-fearing folks. Then you can add a couple of guard towers and searchlights and the effect will be complete. The neighbors will love you. But you won't have those nasty bobcats to worry about.

Seriously—I have heard one anecdotal report of a foothills resident, who had a female bobcat with kittens in her backyard, who called the Game and Fish Department because the bobcat hissed at her when she went outside. Personally, I'd be delighted to have a bobcat with kittens hiss at me, and delighted to share my yard with her. I hope you would be too.

Mountain Lions

It was a late afternoon in July, with the temperature close to one hundred degrees, and my wife and I were driving up the remote dirt road to the house we were caretaking in Brown Canyon, in the Baboquivari Mountains. Both of us spotted the broad scrape mark across the road, and instantly recognized it as evidence that a mountain lion had killed something and dragged it off under cover somewhere. We parked and got out, and found not-yet-coagulated blood drops in the dirt. We followed the drag mark and discovered the warm carcass of a white-tailed doe—a favorite food of mountain lions—under a mesquite tree. It was a classic lion kill: moved under cover, then opened up at the belly, with lots of deer hair scattered around where the cat had licked it from the carcass.

Roseann offered to drive the rest of the way to the house and get the camera, while I waited and investigated the scene. Knowing the lion would have certainly fled at the sound of the truck, I began to poke around beyond the tree, dropping to my hands and knees to get under an acacia. Still kneeling, I looked ahead—and there was the lion, crouched under another shrub no more than fifteen feet away. The instant our eyes made contact, she turned and simply vanished, so quickly and silently that I actually crawled over and verified her tracks to convince myself I hadn't imagined her yellow eyes looking into mine. I recognized the distinctive prints of the resident female we had spotted several times, who had in fact once left dusty pad marks across the length of our porch while we slept.

The point of the story is this: Mountain lions, under virtually all circumstances, are afraid of humans and will not challenge them, even when the human is dumb enough to get between them and a minutes-old kill. Researchers have told me of handling mountain lion kittens to weigh and mark them, while the mother sat in a tree, growling but making no move to attack.

When mountain lions do attack humans, the circumstances often fall into predictable patterns. First, many seem to occur on children or women, probably because their size better fits within the normal range of mountain lion prey (white-tailed deer usually weigh between 70 and 170 pounds). Second, many attacks occur on *moving* victims—runners or even bicyclists—leading to speculation that the animal's chase instincts short-circuit its usual caution. You know what happens when a domestic cat spots a bird hopping along the ground: It adopts a quivering, almost stupid sort of tunnel vision. Other attacks have happened to people who were crouching or sitting, so they might not have been readily identifiable as human.

In other words, a good percentage of mountain lion attacks on humans seem to be a case of mistaken identity. Virtually all attacks are broken off if the victim yells and fights back, further evidence that the cat might not have been aware of the identity of the prey.

However, there is little doubt that at least some lion attacks on humans are purely opportunistic: The lion simply went after what came by. This situation is the most frightening, since it flies in the face of how a lot of animal rights activists like to portray mountain lions. The fact is, they are magnificent and powerful predators quite capable of killing an adult human. The further fact is that as long as our expanding urban areas continue to impinge upon mountain lion territory, we can continue to expect occasional attacks on humans.

Contributing to the problems caused by urban expansion is the mountain lion's life history. Mountain lions are solitary animals, except for brief periods when a male and female are together to mate—which can occur at any time of year but usually peaks in winter—and when a female has young (usually two), which might stay with her for up to twenty-four months. A lion's territory in Arizona can encompass as much as one hundred square miles, and while a female's territory often overlaps those of several males, males do not share space and will fight to the death to defend their own. Thus young male lions are often pushed out to the edges of viable territory by established resident males, and have a difficult time finding enough natural food. When an inexperienced, half-starved lion crosses paths with a jogger, the chances for trouble increase significantly.

What does this portend to a homeowner on the edge of mountain lion habitat? Essentially, nothing.

You must understand the reality behind the statistics. In the entire United States, about one person every three years is killed by a mountain lion, and that has come about only in the last couple of decades. Before that, mountain lion fatalities were nearly unheard of. There are also about a dozen nonfatal attacks each year. By contrast, every year in the United States, around one hundred people are killed when their cars collide with deer. Do you worry every time you drive through the countryside that you might hit a deer and be killed? I don't either. One might make a valid case that many lives could be saved if we had more mountain lions around to keep down the deer population. You are thirty times more likely to be killed by your neighbor's *dog* than by a mountain lion.

Nevertheless, with *intelligent* use of the statistics we have at our disposal, it's perfectly acceptable to consider a few dos and don'ts for mountain lion country, to render the slim chance for a problem even slimmer:

1. Since many attacks have been on children, or groups of children with no adults present, experts suggest, logically, that you not let children under the age of ten or so play alone, or in small groups without an adult around, where mountain lions are known to be resident.
2. If you are threatened by a mountain lion, react aggressively. Do not turn away or run. Wave your arms and yell. If you are attacked, fight back. Mountain lions virtually always retreat in the face of aggression. Do *not* get confused and use this advice when you visit Montana and find yourself between a mother grizzly bear and her cubs.
3. Don't bend over to pick up a rock or stick to throw, as that makes your silhouette look more like prey (Hmm . . . remember the position I was in when I spotted the lion in the beginning of this section?).

In Brown Canyon, Roseann, who weighs 110 pounds, jogged regularly along the same roads where we frequently found lion tracks. Why? First, we were in the middle of ideal lion habitat, meaning there was plenty of natural food around. Second, she always ran with our dog (on a leash), and healthy mountain lions retain an instinctive wariness of dogs. Finally, and most important, she simply recognized the odds against running into trouble. Still, on one occasion, she stopped to re-tie her shoe (thus *crouching,* see number three above), and looked up in time to see a mountain lion stroll across the road about one hundred feet in front of her, completely ignorant of her presence. She looked at the dog, who was watching her, completely ignorant of the mountain lion's presence. So much for the finely tuned senses of wild beasts and man's best friend.

Perhaps the biggest danger to our reasoned relationship with mountain lions is the media, and its natural tendency to sensationalize—followed by the natural human tendency to freak out under media influence. Which headline is an editor more likely to pick to run in big type?: ANOTHER JOG-GER KILLED BY MOUNTAIN LION or FIRST MOUNTAIN LION FATALITY IN THREE YEARS. The idea of being attacked by a wild animal probably speaks to some deep genetic memory within us, enhancing the tendency toward hysteria.

Since mountain lions have virtually no natural predators, the inflexible conundrum presented by mountain lion territory needs versus human encroachment is best addressed through, first, the protection of natural lion habitat and, second, controlled hunting. Like it or not, we need to maintain mountain lion numbers at a steady level to prevent both human-lion problems and the simple hardships faced by any overpopulated species. The professional lion hunters I have met are without exception passionately committed to ensuring the long-term survival of the species. While such an attitude is incomprehensible to many, it works. Scientific management of mountain lion populations, including hunting, will ensure that the general public's benign attitude toward mountain lions remains that way.

The true test of our willingness to share this planet with other animals will come with those species that extract a cost from us for our largesse. It's easy to coo over warblers and dolphins and koalas. Will our beneficence stop with those animals that are convenient to have around? Or will we continue to display the sense of honor that allows us to include species that might compete with us or even, on rare occasions, harm us? I hope we will.

10

And Finally, the Creepy Crawlies

That's *arthropods* to you illuminatti.

Scientists have calculated that for every human on earth there are approximately forty thousand pounds of arthropods (a term that means "jointed foot," and applies to insects, arachnids, and many other classes of "bugs," as well as crustaceans such as lobsters). That statistic seems less outrageous in southern Arizona, where we obviously have, at the very least, zillions of them. The vast majority are not only perfectly harmless, but utterly irreplaceable (if all arthropods suddenly disappeared from the earth, most other life would also disappear within weeks). Many are beautiful even to non-bug-lovers. But a few can cause problems beyond an attack of the "eeeews."

It's ironic that the smallest creatures produce some of the most potent emotions, but, to be fair, we do have some quite splendidly fearsome looking arthropods in southern Arizona, some of which can hurt us. And even the most tolerant and enthusiastic naturalists have limits.

I remember one house Roseann and I lived in far out in the desert, that appeared to be smack in the middle of God's own scorpion factory, the little *Centruroides* species, or bark scorpions, the ones that hurt like blazes when they sting. They're also the only scorpion prone to climbing, which was a real problem in this house, as it had not only rough plaster interior walls, but rough-cut pine plank ceilings. It was disconcerting to be reading in bed and glance up to see a little yellow scorpion trundling along upside down directly above your face. You couldn't help but wonder, what happens if it *trips?*

For the first few months in this house I was unbelievably diligent in capturing every scorpion in the house and letting it go outside (we're talking *every night* here, sometimes two or three individuals). But eventually the repetition of getting up just short of sleep to corral a ceiling-roving scorpion, then taking it outside in my underwear (thus quadrupling my chances of an encounter with one of its relatives) became too much, and I began employing a different tool: a long walking staff with a big rubber tip. Didn't even have to get out of bed.

Kissing Bugs

I employed the Terminal Solution on scorpions with some regret, but gleefully dealt out death to another summer invader: cone-nosed bugs, also known disarmingly as kissing bugs. These little blood-sucking devils, uh, I mean, insects, are normally associated with woodrats, but would feed on us or our dog any time they got the chance, leaving a nasty, itching red welt on our leg or arm that would last for a week, and making our dog seriously ill. A mosquito net hung over the bed kept most of them out, but I'd often awake to see one clinging to the netting, eyeing us greedily. I always resisted the temptation to pull off its wings and piercing proboscis and four or five legs and let it go, instead merely administering a quick smash. But not without a cackle of satisfaction. Fortunately for those of us in cone-nosed territory, their season is short—May into August.

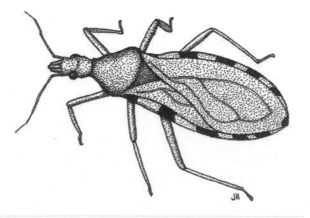

A cone-nosed bug
(*Triatoma* sp.).

Scorpions

Scorpions are undoubtedly our most feared arthropod. They are arachnids, rather distantly related to spiders. Arizona has many species, but three of them are known to most longtime residents: The bark scorpion *(Centruroides exilicauda)*, which I already mentioned, only a couple of inches long and very slender; a slightly larger one called the stripe-tailed *(Vaejovis spinigeris)*; and the giant hairy scorpion *(Hadrurus arizonensis)*. The latter *is* big, up to four inches long or so, and hairy too, but its sting is the mildest of the bunch, often compared to a bee or wasp sting. The bark scorpion's sting, on the other hand, hurts like hell for what seems like months (actually up to twenty-four hours or so).

In reality, it's pretty darn difficult to get stung by a scorpion if you just *watch where you put your bare feet and hands.* In fact, every single person I've known who's been stung got it when they ignored or forgot this axiom. Bark scorpions do sometimes climb into clothing, but you can prevent that by keeping your hanging clothes away from walls. And yes, they do occasionally show up in shoes.

If you need to evict a scorpion from a building, catching it is easy, since they tend to sit still unless you molest them. Whether the scorpion is on a wall or the floor, just place a glass jar (which makes it easier to see what you're doing) over it, then slide a piece of thin cardboard underneath and upend it.

Finding scorpions outdoors is easy with a battery-operated ultraviolet lamp, since they fluoresce a beautiful yellow-greenish hue. But I've horrified more than a few people by showing them just how many scorpions were hanging around their houses at night. It's a natural human tendency to react thusly, instead of being logical and thinking, *Wow, if there have been that many around all this time and I've never been stung, it must be really unusual to have trouble.*

Centipedes

Another local arthropod with an overblown reputation is the centipede. Certainly, if looks could kill, a big ten-inch-long desert centipede would do so, but actually very few people are bitten (centipedes bite—more or less—with a modified pair of legs; scorpions sting), and those who have been

report only the proverbial wasp-sting-like pain. Centipedes are retiring and
nocturnal, and don't normally wind up where you can put your hand on one
or even step on one. If you did, it would have a difficult time bringing its
biting parts, which are on its underside, to bear before you leapt off screech-
ing. Centipedes were one of the few things I didn't try to pick up barehanded
as a kid, because I was told *all* their legs carried venom—a myth. (By the way,
I discovered that picking up *scorpions* is easy: You just have to move quickly
and pinch their stinger between thumb and forefinger. But don't try this at
home.)

Spiders

We have two spiders that can inflict painful bites: the ubiquitous black
widow and the Arizona brown spider (there are actually about five very
similar species). Our brown spider is closely related to but not the same
species as the brown recluse. Neither the black widow nor the brown spider is a threat to life, and both are very shy. Bites are uncommon. Most of
the spiders you see around your home are far more harmless hunting or web-
spinning spiders. I run a constant personal crusade to convince people to
leave spiders alone, or at least to move them outside. They are extremely
beneficial at controlling the population of a lot of smaller things you don't
want around.

   A spider that rarely shows up in houses is the tarantula. Looking like the
offspring of a normal spider and a fairly good-sized mouse, tarantula males
are frequently spotted roaming the desert on summer evenings, looking for
females, which stick close to their burrows and await suitors like prim Vic-
torian maidens. At least, they're prim until the actual consummation of the
courtship occurs. Then the male, who must position himself under the female to transfer sperm, has to use a special set of hooks on his front legs to
hold the female's fangs away from him. When he is finished he bails out and
runs like hell.

   To humans, tarantulas—even females—are utterly harmless. Yes, they can
inflict a mildly painful bite, but you would have to seriously harass one to
produce such a reaction. More annoying to some people are the barbed hairs
that grow on the spider's abdomen, which readily come loose and can cause
irritation, especially if one gets in your eye.

   Tarantulas have overcome their fearsome reputation for all but the most

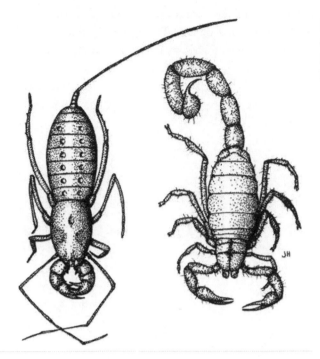

Left: a whipscorpion,
or vinegaroon.
Right: a giant hairy
scorpion.

helpless arachnophobes. The females actually make great, long-lived (ten years or more) pets, feeding readily on grasshoppers and other insects. Males die much sooner, undoubtedly from hypertension.

Sun Spiders and Whipscorpions

A couple of other local arachnids have the capability of striking terror into those who spot them, despite being completely harmless. Solpugids, also called sun spiders, are heavy-bodied things about two inches long with a huge, evil-looking pincher assembly on the head. They can run at about one-quarter light speed, which doesn't help their reputation, but they do no harm except to your equanimity if one happens to vector in your direction while attempting to escape. Then it's difficult to resist the urge to leap onto the nearest piece of furniture.

Much bigger—like, *huge*—but just as harmless, is the whipscorpion, which looks startlingly like a giant hairy scorpion, except that its eponymous tail is a long, horsehair-thin appendage with no stinger. Whipscorpions are also called vinegaroons because their chief defense is to squirt an acidic substance out the rear of the abdomen. This, and their resemblance to real scorpions, probably helps whipscorpions avoid predation in many instances. Unfortunately the latter trait works against them around humans, where the usual result is that the poor thing suddenly assumes a stature about one-tenth its former height and occupies considerably more floor space, while the human inspects the bottom of his or her shoe and says, "Oh, *yuck!*"

Bug Tolerance

The traditional approach to dealing with bugs around the home has been to sign up for a monthly dousing with chemicals from a pest control company. A relative of mine who shall remain further unidentified has subscribed to one such service for at least thirty years, despite my pleas. That the service works on at least one level is beyond doubt—she finds dead bugs everywhere. The odd thing is, she also constantly finds *live* bugs everywhere, convincing her that the monthly spraying is all the more vital. I've never been able to convince her that the live bugs are just immigrants taking the place of the dead ones, a cycle that will continue for infinity or until her pest company owner retires to the Bahamas on a fifty-foot sailboat. The population of live bugs in her house is no greater, and definitely no lower, than the natural level I have experienced living in several remote houses, none of which ever benefited from a single application of chemicals. Remember the principle I mentioned earlier: If you kill something that has a natural population in the area, another is *certain* to take its place. Given this questionable efficacy, the cost involved, and the possible effects on birds and other animals that eat the poisoned bugs around your home, it's worthwhile seriously debating whether to adopt such a generalized antibug strategy, or to just address specific problems when they arise.

A great book about southwestern arthropods is *Insects of the Southwest,* by Floyd Werner and Carl Olson. How these two acquiesced to titling the book *Insects of the Southwest,* when at least a third of the entries are not insects, is a mystery. Most likely some dour-faced marketing director at their press insisted that *Insects, Arachnids, Crustacea, Diplopods, and Chilopods of the Southwest* just wouldn't sell. In any case, the book is a trove of information about everything from scorpions to butterflies.

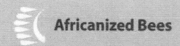

Africanized Bees

I can't remember a "natural" event that was anticipated with as much speculation, fear, and fear-mongering, as the arrival of Africanized bees in Arizona. Now that we've had a decade to live with them, it's safe to draw a few conclusions.

The familiar European honeybee *(Apis melifera)* was introduced to the New World by the Spanish, possibly as early as the 1500s. The species quickly spread across the continent and is now ubiquitous, playing an incalculably vital role in the pollenization of thousands of species of wild plants and domestic crops. It's been estimated that one-third of U.S. food production depends directly on bees, and that's not counting the 275 million pounds of honey we consume each year. Ecologically, the impact of the European honeybee is less clear, although it's known they outcompete native bees in certain areas.

In 1956, a scientist in Brazil imported colonies of an African race of *A. melifera* to experiment with cross-breeding, in an attempt to create a honeybee strain better suited to tropical conditions. Some of the queens escaped and began a fantastically successful hybridization conquest of the existing, "native" honeybee population. The Africanized strain has been spreading northward ever since, and reached the United States in Texas in 1990, gaining a foothold in Arizona three years later. Arizona's first death from Africanized bees occurred in October 1993; since then there have been seven additional deaths.

Southern Arizona is now, as far as we can foresee, a permanent home for Africanized bees. It is not known how much farther north they will expand; most scientists believe the strain has a cold tolerance limit that will eventually stop them.

Africanized bees are outwardly remarkably similar to a standard European honeybee; it takes an expert to distinguish them. Africanized bees do not have more potent venom or more of it; a single sting feels just like an ordinary sting. What sets the hybridized strain apart is its significantly heightened aggression, particularly near the hive. Africanized bees are more likely to attack a perceived threat, more of them are likely to respond, and they are more likely to follow a fleeing threat farther than other bees. Many victims have been doing something such as mowing a lawn, the noise (and, reportedly, the *smell*) of which apparently aggravated the bees, but others have done nothing but walk too close to a hive. The result can be dozens or even hundreds of stings.

So, sadly, southern Arizona residents must now treat all bee hives, both in town and in the wild, with healthy suspicion. Note, however, that

Africanized bees appear to be no more aggressive than other bees when foraging or watering, so you don't have to worry about the bees you see on your flowers, hummingbird feeders, or birdbaths. What you need to watch for are signs of a hive: clusters of bees around small (often under a half-inch in diameter) holes or cracks, behind which might be larger spaces suitable for comb building. If you find such evidence, keep yourself and your pets away from it, and call a bee removal expert. Obviously, a preventive approach is best, so inspect your home for possible entrances and block them off with caulking or foam sealant.

Incidentally, there is a difference between a bee hive and a swarm. A hive is a more or less permanent residence that bees will defend. A swarm is a tightly packed cluster of several thousand bees and a queen that is searching for a new hive site. Most swarming occurs in spring or early summer. A swarm will often be out in the open, for example, hanging off a tree limb,

Bee swarms, such as this one in a mesquite, are looking for a new hive site and will leave soon. There's no need to take action.

while scouts look for a promising site. Such a phenomenon is temporary—it's certain they'll be gone in anywhere from a few hours to a couple of days, so no action is needed. Swarming bees are generally nonaggressive.

Experts suggest several things to do if you are attacked by bees. First, if possible, get inside a car, building, or even a tent, and close the entrances. Do not jump into a pool of water, as the bees will wait for you to surface. If no shelter is nearby, *run*. A human can normally outrun a group of bees, although Africanized bees are likely to pursue you for several hundred yards. If possible, cover your face, since it is the most dangerous area for stings, even if you have to lift your shirt over your head and suffer more stings on your torso. If possible, avoid swatting, since the smell of dead bees will only further aggravate the survivors.

If you have pets, make sure they have a safe place to escape to if they are attacked while you're not nearby. Several dogs have been killed by bees when left staked out in a yard by their owners.

Overall, the dangers from Africanized bees are easy to exaggerate. As with most such potential hazards, knowledge and awareness are your best defenses.

I hope, after reading both this section and Werner and Olson's book, that you'll be more favorably inclined to show forbearance to all the little skittering things that wander into our lives from the surrounding desert. You're allowed to have an exception or two (like me and those cone-nosed bugs), but you'll be surprised at how satisfying it is to forge a truce with the arthropod world.

In fact, my hope with this whole chapter is that you'll extend that forbearance to all those animals that share space with us in southern Arizona. Remember that we impact their lives, with our developments, our roads and cars, our pesticides, far more disastrously than they do ours by waking us up early or nesting in our storerooms or even eating our pets now and then. Before you get annoyed at the next woodpecker or javelina or rattlesnake, stop and think for a minute. You'll be surprised at how thin the line often is between annoyance and amusement. Once you decide to be amused rather than annoyed, you can go back to enjoying the incredible variety of wildlife that graces southern Arizona.

Afterword
Preserving Habitat and Connections

One encounters strident emotions and conflicting perceptions when discussing the development that has devoured thousands of acres of desert in the last decades.

Virtually all conservationists agree that, if development must occur, it's better to cluster it and leave open space for habitat and wildlife. For example, if you have one thousand undisturbed acres on which to build housing for two hundred families, it's preferable to mark off fifty acres, build your two hundred homes there on quarter-acre lots, and leave nine hundred and fifty acres as open space and habitat, than to cover the entire one thousand acres with five-acre "ranchettes." The latter, low-density style of development, while it creates the appearance of openness around each home, is actually much worse for the wildlife, which must run a gauntlet of roads, cars, dogs and cats, noise, and pesticides dispersed across the entire area. Many large mammals simply can't survive in such conditions; those one thousand acres are essentially lost to them as habitat. Only at even lower densities—one house per twenty or forty acres—is it possible to consider the habitat somewhat intact, with large animals moving through or foraging without undue disturbance.

Tragically, what happens all too commonly in southern Arizona is that the entire one thousand acres is diced into quarter-acre lots, and four thousand families move in.

But we seem to be moving, however slowly, toward a realistic approach

Without enough habitat protected from vehicles and development, our wildlife faces a dim future.

to providing living space for humans while also providing it for wildlife. Much of this approach involves the concepts I've discussed earlier, of wildlife movement corridors connecting large islands of undisturbed habitat. Politicians are beginning to realize, or admit, that a vast majority of the American public, regardless of political affiliation, strongly supports the idea of setting aside land for wildlife. They know that that land is also set aside for them and for their children, to enjoy the outdoors and the animals that live there. This preference holds true even when participants in polls are asked if they would accept higher taxes as the price for preserving open space.

In southern Arizona, particularly, we are beginning to realize the fallacy of the theory that "growth pays for itself." A recent study revealed that every new home built outside the city limits requires something like twenty thousand dollars in expenditures for capital improvements such as new roads and traffic controls, plumbing and sewage treatment, electricity, and services such as schools, sanitation, and law enforcement. Traditionally, these costs have been borne by those already living here, many of whom don't want the new growth anyway. Now our willingness to allow uncontrolled expansion of new development is fading.

The development that does still occur can be done in ways to minimize destruction of habitat, while concurrently creating a more pleasant place to live and increasing the value of the homes within it. Open space preservation is key to this, as are protected corridors along natural movement pathways such as washes. Promoting native landscaping rather than lawns and hedges and golf courses helps at the microhabitat level, and conserves water for the entire community.

Also vital to intelligent development is recognizing where it shouldn't be allowed at all. Presently, our only effective weapon in this struggle is the Endangered Species Act, which requires designation of critical habitat for certain at-risk species. Although anyone who thinks about it realizes that habitat set aside for one species actually benefits hundreds of others as well, it is perhaps time for a new approach, one that considers the entire diversity and uniqueness of a landscape rather than focusing on one entity.

What we are realizing most strongly in recent years is the need to find *permanent* ways to safeguard large, intact natural landscapes and the corridors that connect them, rather than just postponing their destruction. Far from being an antipeople movement, as its detractors like to claim, this movement is in fact vigorously propeople, recognizing the desire to ensure our children the same connection to the natural world we and our parents enjoyed.

One gratifying recent phenomenon is the breakdown of barriers between special interest groups who share overall goals but different philosophies. For years ranchers were pitted against environmentalists, who were pitted against hunters, who were against the ranchers. Recently, all have begun to realize that fragmentation and loss of habitat is the real evil, and that whether cows are on it or hunting is allowed is a small consideration next to its potential total disappearance. The first time I sat down at a table with a vegetarian on one side of me and a professional mountain lion hunter on the other, and we all agreed to work together, was when I started realizing we can win.

While the main battle lines might seem to be at the point where bulldozer meets virgin desert, there are many more modest ways to preserve habitat and connections within already existing neighborhoods. Even in the middle of town, for example, our university-area community waged a so-far-successful battle to keep High School Wash from being bladed, channelized, and concreted into just another culvert devoid of beauty or life. The supposed justification for the channelization was "flood control," even though it has been proved that such projects do nothing but increase the velocity of flood waters, thus actually exacerbating problems downstream. Sometimes bureaucracies lack not only any aesthetic sense, but basic knowledge of science and engineering as well.

It doesn't matter if you're a native or yesterday's immigrant, whether you live in a midtown condo or on a cattle ranch, whether you eat tofu or hunt your own venison, you can still make your voice heard in the fight to preserve habitat and wildlife. Please speak loudly and often.

Appendix 1
Butterfly Plants

#	Botanical Name	Common Name	Nectar/ Larval	Flower Season	Comments
1	*Pithecellobium flexicaule*	Texas Ebony	N, L	S	Frost hardy; evergreen
2	*Caesalpinia pulcherrima*	Mexican Red Bird-of-Paradise	N	S,F	Also attracts hummingbirds
3	*Dalea lutea*	Indigo Bush	L	F	Yellow-flowered shrub
4	*Dalea capitata*	Indigo Bush	N	Sp,F	Groundcover
5	*Lantana camara*	Lantana "Miss Huff"	N	Sp,S,F	Frost tender
6	*Lantana camara*	Lantana "Radiation"	N	Sp,S,F	Tropical origin
7	*Lantana camara*	Lantana "Dallas Red"	N	Sp,S,F	Ornamental shrub
8	*Lantana camara*	Yellow Lantana	N	Sp,S,F	Variable growth forms
9	*Lantana montevidensis*	Purple Trailing Lantana	N	Sp,S,F	Groundcover
10	*Lantana montevidensis*	White Trailing Lantana	N	Sp,S,F	Groundcover
11	*Achillea millefolium*	"Fuerland" Yarrow	N	Sp	Mountain meadow origin
12	*Achillea millefolium*	"Summer Wine" Yarrow	N	Sp	Cultivar variability
13	*Chilopsis linearis*	Desert Willow	N, L	S,F	Sphinx moth larval food
14	*Tithonia fruticosa*	Mexican Sunflower	N	Sp,F	Large, perennial shrub
15	*Cosmos cultivars*	Cosmos	N	Sp,S,F	Warm season annual

#	Botanical Name	Common Name	Nectar/ Larval	Flower Season	Comments
16	*Sambucus mexicana*	Mexican Elderberry	N	Sp	Winter-spring grower
17	*Celtis pallida*	Desert Hackberry	L	S	Snout and brush-footed
18	*Senna leucosperma*	Tree Senna	L	S,F	Frost tender
19	*Senna occidentalis*	Senna or Cassia	L	F	Small shrub
20	*Lycium brevipes*	Baja Wolfberry	N	W,Sp	Winter-spring grower
21	*Calliandra eriophylla*	Fairy Duster	N, L	Sp,F	Attractive low shrub
22	*Lycium species*	Wolfberry	N	W, Sp	Slow growing
23	*Rhamnus californica*	California Buck Thorn	N, L	Sp	Large, evergreen shrub
24	*Eupatorium greggii*	Thoroughwort	N	S,F	Perennial herb
25	*Citharexylum flabellifolium*	Shrub Verbena	N	Sp,S	Medium, woody shrub
26	*Ageratum coryumbosum*	Flossflower	N	S,F	Perennial herb
27	*Mimosa dysocarpa*	Velvet Pod Mimosa	N	S,F	Pink and white flowers
28	*Senna wislizenii*	Senna or Cassia	L	F	3–4 foot, woody shrub
29	*Senna purpusii*	Senna or Cassia	L	W,Sp	Tender; blue-green leaves
30	*Senna covesii*	Senna or Cassia	L	F	Attracts Sulphur butterflies
31	*Glandularia gooddingii*	Gooding's Verbena	N	Sp,S	Winter-spring grower
32	*Bahia absinthifolia*	Bahia	N	Sp,F	Small; sunflower family
33	*Bouteloua curtipendula*	Sideoats Grama	L	S,F	Attracts Queen butterflies
34	*Heteropogon contortus*	Tanglehead Grass	L	S,F	Attracts Queen butterflies
35	*Calliandra californica*	Baja Fairy Duster	N, L	Sp,S,F,W	Also attracts hummingbirds
36	*Marina parryi*	Indigo Bush	L	Sp,F	Low groundcover

#	Botanical Name	Common Name	Nectar/ Larval	Flower Season	Comments
37	*Chrysothamnus nauseosus*	Rabbitbrush	N	F,W	Chaparral origin
38	*Sphaeralcea ambigua*	Desert Mallow	L	Sp	Attracts Skipper butterflies
39	*Dalea pulchra*	Indigo Bush	L	Sp	Attracts Sulphur butterflies
40	*Dalea bicolor*	Indigo Bush	L	F	Also attracts Dogface
41	*Dyssodia pentachaeta*	Dogweed or Dyssodia	L	Sp,S,F	Attracts Orange-tips
42	*Dalea frutescens*	Indigo Bush	L	Sp,F	Small, purple flowers
43	*Plumbago scandens*	Plumbago	N	Sp,F	Frost tender
44	*Prosopis velutina*	Velvet Mesquite	L	Sp,F	Attracts Blues & Hairstreaks
45	*Hesperaloe nocturna*	Hesperaloe	N	Sp	Accent plant
46	*Telosiphonia nacapulensis*	Nacapule Rock Trumpet	N	S,F	Fragrant, white flowers
47	*Telosiphonia brachysiphon*	Rock Trumpet	N	S,F	Attracts Sphinx moth
48	*Gaura lindheimeri*	Gaura	N	Sp	Tubular, pink flower
49	*Calylophus hartwegii*	Yellow Evening-Primrose	N	Sp,F	Attracts Sphinx moth
50	*Oenothera caespitosa*	Tufted Evening-Primrose	N, L	Sp	Heart-shaped, white petals
51	*Oenothera hookeri*	Hooker's Evening-Primrose	N	Sp	Yellow flowers
52	*Datura quercifolia*	Oak Leaf Thorn-Apple	L	Sp,S	Attracts Sphinx moth
53	*Datura wrightii*	Thorn-Apple or Jimson Weed	L	Sp,S	Attracts Sphinx moth
54	*Mirabilis longiflora*	Four-o'Clock	N	Sp	20–30 foot vine
55	*Mirabilis multiflora*	Four-o'Clock	N	Sp	Large, purple flowers
56	*Coreopsis bigelovii*	Desert Coreopsis	N	W,Sp	Annual; yellow flowers
57	*Zinnia grandiflora*	Prairie Zinnia	N	S,F	Low groundcover

#	Botanical Name	Common Name	Nectar/ Larval	Flower Season	Comments
58	*Streptanthus carinatus*	Silverbells	L	Sp	Annual; white flowers
59	*Cosmos sulfureus*	Cosmos	N	S,F	3–5 foot annual; orange flowers

Appendix 2
Hummingbird Plants

	Botanical Name	Common Name		Botanical Name	Common Name
1	*Aloe barbadensis*	Aloe vera	17	*Fouquieria diguetii*	Mexican Tree Ocotillo
2	*Aloe bellatula*	Aloe	18	*Galvezia juncea*	Galvezia
3	*Agave polyanthiflora*		19	*Hamelia patens*	Fire Bush
4	*Aloe massawana*	Aloe	20	*Hesperaloe nocturna*	White Hesperaloe
5	*Anisacanthus andersonii*		21	*Hesperaloe parviflora*	Red Hesperaloe
6	*Anisacanthus quadrifidus var. wrightii*	Desert Honey-suckle cv. Mexican Flame	22	*Justicia candicans*	Red Jacobinia
7	*Anisacanthus thurberi*	Desert Honey-suckle	23	*Justicia sonorae*	Purple Jacobinia
8	*Aquilegia chrysantha*	Golden Columbine	24	*Justicia spicigera*	Orange Jacobinia
9	*Hesperaloe parviflora "Yellow"*	Yellow Hesperaloe	25	*Karwinskia humboldtiana*	
10	*Calliandra californica*	Baja Fairy Duster	26	*Lobelia cardinalis*	Cardinal Flower
11	*Calliandra eriophylla*	Fairy Duster	27	*Lobelia laxiflora*	Lobelia
12	*Mammillaria poselgeri*	Pincushion Cactus	28	*Mammillaria setispina*	Pincushion Cactus
13	*Mammillaria maritima*	Pincushion Cactus	29	*Mimulus cardinalis*	Red Monkey Flower
14	*Eriogonum fasciculatum*	Flattop Buckwheat	30	*Pedilanthus macrocarpus*	Slipper Flower
15	*Erythrina flabelliformis*	Southwest Coral Bean	31	*Penstemon eatonii*	Firecracker Penstemon
16	*Echinocereus pensilis*	Snake Cactus	32	*Russelia furfuracea*	Russelia
			33	*Salvia greggii cv. Furman's Red*	Red Autumn Sage

	Botanical Name	Common Name		Botanical Name	Common Name
34	*Ruellia peninsularis*	Ruellia	43	*Zauschneria californica* var. *latifolia*	Hummingbird Trumpet
35	*Salvia mohavensis*	Mohave Sage			
36	*Salvia x cv. Carl Nielsen*	Carl Nielsen Sage	44	*Monarda austro-montanus*	Bee Balm
37	*Stenocereus alamosensis*	Sina	45	*Eremophila decipiens*	
38	*Tecoma garrocha*	Orange Bells	46	*Aloe cv. Lizard lips*	Aloe
39	*Tecoma stans* var. *angustata*	Arizona Yellow Bells	47	*Aloe parvula x aristata*	Aloe
40	*Tecoma stans* var. *stans*	Broadleaf Yellow Bells	48	*Aloe humilis x pictifolia*	Aloe
41	*Penstemon cardinalis*	Cardinal Penstemon	49	*Heuchera sanguinea*	Coral Bells
42	*Lonicera sempervirens*	Desert Honey-suckle Vine			

Index

About the Author

Writer and naturalist Jonathan Hanson was born in Tucson and has lived and worked in several remote locations in southern Arizona. He is the author of nearly a dozen books on natural history and outdoor sports, several of them collaborations with his wife, Roseann. He is a correspondent for *Outside* magazine and has written for many others, including *Nature Conservancy* and *National Geographic Adventure*. Jonathan teaches a variety of subjects, such as animal tracking, birding, and nature writing for several conservation organizations. He and his wife currently live in the Sierrita Mountains southwest of Tucson.